Silk Bonsai

Silk Bonsai

PATRICIA RATCLIFFE

Dryad Press Ltd
London

Dedication

To my grandchildren – Helen, Claire,
Victoria and Daniel

Acknowledgement

My grateful thanks to my friends Nancy
Greenway and Magda Ounsworth for their
encouragement and advice, and to my
students, for without their terrific
enthusiasm and constant requests for
something new I would never have
attempted this book. Also to Jeff Brook-
Smith for the artwork and to Keith John
Heppell for the photography.

ISBN 0 8521 97063

Typeset by Keyspools Ltd, Golborne, Lancs
and printed in Great Britain by
Anchor Brendon Ltd
Tiptree, Essex
for the publishers
Dryad Press Ltd
8 Cavendish Square
London W1M 0AJ

Contents

Useful information   87

Introduction

For many years I made only silk flowers; then, at the flower and horticultural shows I visited for inspiration, I first noticed and then became fascinated by bonsai. Some I found grotesque, but the graceful shapes and proportionate foliage of others seemed quite delightful. The idea of creating 'silk' bonsai only occurred to me later, after I had been teaching silk flowermaking for some time. To see how it could be done I began to research the subject. I discovered that there are very clear rules for the proportioning of bonsai and I realized that the rules that apply to live bonsai would serve equally well for the silk variety.

First we need to learn what exactly is 'bonsai'. The word bonsai actually means 'grown in a shallow dish', but it is used to describe miniature trees that are kept small by careful training and pruning of both branches and roots. Some of these trees live to a great age. The word is also used for a single tree.

And now a brief word about this book, and a word of advice. The first chapter deals with the equipment and materials you will need and suitable containers, and gives rules and styles for bonsai in general. The methods for forming the parts of the tree are described in the following chapter. Then step-by-step instructions are given for sixteen types of bonsai, beginning with a small but pleasing willow and working up through several different styles to larger and more complicated projects. In each case illustrations and lists of materials are given. Ideally the craft worker should have some experience of silk flowermaking, and it is advised that even then a small tree is attempted to begin with.

I hope that you will find all the trees as fascinating to make as I did to design, and, having mastered the technique of making them with the help of this book, will go on to further creation, using books on live bonsai and nature itself for inspiration.

Chapter I

Before you begin

Equipment

Expensive equipment is not necessary; a sharp medium-sized pair of scissors, wire cutters and long-nosed pliers are all the tools required. A flower iron is useful but not essential. Other useful items are:

Kitchen roll or toilet tissue

Kitchen foil

Texturing powder from a model shop

Dry hard florist's clay

Reindeer moss or dried lichen

Cold water wallpaper paste

Glue size

Fine peat and gravel

Dry oasis

Plaster of paris or polyfilla

Matt brown paint

Modelling clay ⎫
⎬ for making fruit
Craft paint ⎭

Materials

Specialized Japanese flowermaking ribbon for the flowers and leaves. This ribbon is all 7.2 cm wide

Wires in various gauges

Glue and double-sided tape

Stem tape and bonsai tape

Stamens and berries

The above materials are all available from Hamilworth Floral Products Ltd (see Chapter 4 for the address). Some of the items are obtainable elsewhere but I prefer to use the Japanese materials imported by Hamilworth as I have found them to be the best for the job. The Japanese have other materials at their disposal but as these are not yet obtainable in the UK I have improvised where necessary, as I am sure you will.

Most of the berries and fruit used on the bonsai in this book have been bought but if you are confident about your painting and colouring abilities it is possible to make your own using Das modelling clay and acrylic or enamel paints.

Containers

Traditional bonsai pots are not always easy to find and are expensive. This is because they need to be made from a special type of clay and to be double fired to withstand the pressure from growing roots and freezing temperatures outside. Happily, silk bonsai do not need such specialized containers, so the sort of containers used for floral art may be suitable. It is, however, important that the right shape is chosen for a particular style of bonsai. Generally speaking, for an upright (*chokkan*) or slanting (*shakan*) style the width of the pot should be about one-third the height of the tree. Cascade (*kengai*) and semi-cascade (*hai-kengai*) styles will require a deeper container to balance them. Alternatively the container can be placed on a stand to give the impression of greater depth.

It is a good idea to gradually build up a collection of suitable containers so that you can easily match a particular tree. Indeed, occasionally a particularly pleasing container brings to mind the style of tree to suit it rather than the other way round. The pots I use may not always be authentic but are always carefully chosen to complement the style of bonsai, and have the advantage of being relatively inexpensive.

Shallow dishes from the kitchen or home-made items from the pottery class can all be used. The polystyrene blocks packed around clocks and radios can be textured with plaster and sprayed. Junk shops can often yield shallow serving dishes without lids, plain if possible so as not to detract from the tree. Straight-sided pottery planters and shallow containers from floral art shops, even the humble oasis dish, can be pressed into service given the right treatment.

Personally I prefer not to use plastic containers since, apart from being aesthetically wrong, they do not look or feel solid enough to balance the tree.

Rules to remember

There are several traditional styles for bonsai and any leading book on the subject will show them. As with ikebana, it is important that the rules and styles are adhered to.

Most of the styles I have used are self-explanatory, but *mame bonsai* is one style I think should be mentioned specifically here. A bonsai grown in the mame style is one that is restricted in height to 15 cm or less, including its container.

- A good bonsai should have its roots, trunk, branches, leaves and flowers all in proportion.
- The roots are encouraged to show and should grow in all directions, but they must not cross over each other. They need not be the same thickness or distance apart.
- The shape and appearance of the trunk is very important. It should be clearly visible all the way up, and should taper from the roots to the crown. Trunks may be straight or curved, but in the latter case the curves should look natural and branches should be located on the outer side of the curve, getting smaller towards the top.
- A bonsai has a front and a back and although it should be pleasing to look at from all angles, the larger branches are only allowed to grow towards the rear and sides. For artistic reasons, only in the top part of the tree can small branches and twigs be allowed to grow towards the front. The one exception to this may be a tree grown in the broom style.
- When looking down on a bonsai from above no branch should be at the same height or growing parallel to another and nor should it hide another completely.
- The older the tree appears the more valuable it is, so certain methods are used to age bonsai.

All these rules can be applied to silk bonsai, and we have the added joy of being able to keep our bonsai inside for all to admire. Live bonsai prefer to grow outside and can only be brought inside for two or three weeks at a time.

Chapter 2

Basic techniques

Using the bonsai tape

Where thickness is required, tissue and foil are used to build up each section. Hold each layer in place with ordinary stem tape. Bonsai tape is then used in varying widths for the final layer, and again when the tree is nearing completion. I use 3.6 cm bonsai tape and cut the widths to my requirements. Care must be taken when using bonsai tape to bind firmly, as unlike stem tape it does not stretch and can break.

Forming the branches

When making up branches care should be taken to build up the branch proportionately as you go along, adding an extra layer of tissue or tape if necessary to hide any sudden bumps where wires end.

When instructions say, for instance, 'Thicken for 4 cm to 2 cm across' the thickness should gradually be increased to 2 cm over a length of 4 cm and then be tapered off again to nothing. This same principle will apply when making roots (see section on roots). Remember, the final layer of tape will add another fraction of thickness, so you should err on the thin side of measurements to compensate for this. Extra bulk can always be added at the final texturing.

When using tissue or foil for thickening, stem tape is used between layers to build firm branches, trunks and roots (any coloured or old stem tape can be used up for this purpose).

A final layer of stem tape is also necessary to stop the top layer of bonsai tape slipping.

Branches are formed by first making the flowers, or fruit, and leaves in accordance with the instructions for the appropriate bonsai. Using the diagrams and written instructions, join these together using a full-length piece of tape-covered 18-gauge wire for each section. For small trees a half piece may be used – the pattern will state this where necessary. Use quarter-width bonsai tape for the tips of the branches, and build up any thickness required as the branch gets larger with tissue and stem tape, finishing with half-width bonsai tape.

Try to bend and shape each branch as you go along, keeping the final measurement in mind. Do not clip off any extra length of wire at this stage, as it will be needed to form a firm trunk. Taper the thickness off towards the end of the wire. It is often easier to do some of the texturing at this stage, while the branches are easily handled. The method is described later in the chapter. It is also helpful to make a pen mark on the branches at the lowest measurement given to avoid measuring again when assembling the tree.

To assemble the crown of the tree, correctly position the first two branches to be joined and bind tightly with 28-gauge wire. Twist the ends together and bind any surplus wire down the stem of the branches. Tape firmly with stem tape, thicken if required, and

roots in different sizes

bind together
with wire

FIG. B

FIG. A

bind and tape
18 wires together
above roots

FIG. C

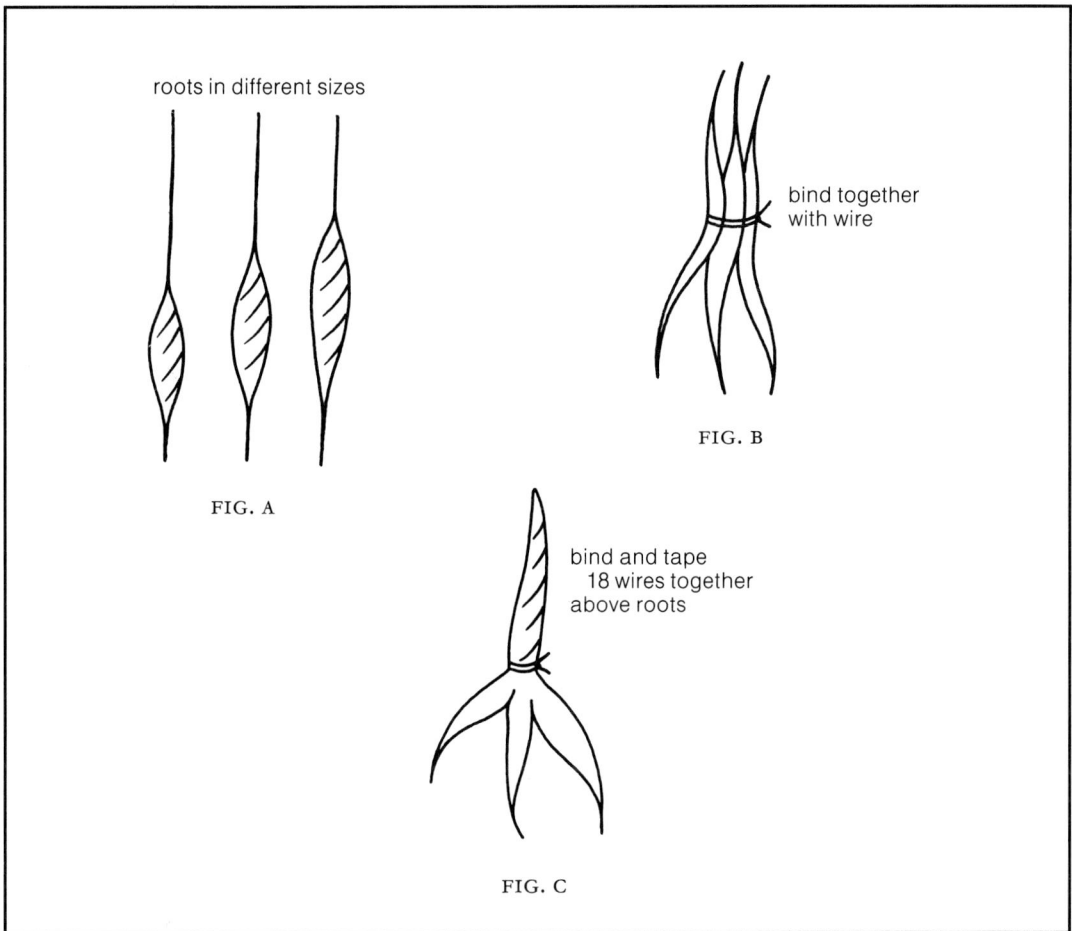

finish with bonsai tape before adding the next branch. Continue until all the top part of the tree has been completed.

Making the roots

Roots on bonsai are meant to be exposed: they form a visual link with the container, and yet must be an integral and balanced part of the beauty of the whole tree. Care and attention must be given to their positions when joining them together and again when joining them to the crown of the tree. The final style of the tree being made, and if possible the shape of the container, must be borne in mind.

To make the roots, first cover a full-length piece of 18-gauge wire with stem tape (half-piece if stated in the pattern). Cut a length of kitchen roll or tissue about 1 inch wide and use it as you would stem tape. Start no more than 2 cm from the end of the wire and build up the thickness to the width and length required, and including the 2 cm tip. Use stem tape between layers of tissue to hold it firm. Taper the roots off above the required measurement (this will help to form the trunk). Finish in bonsai tape. Measure the roots and mark at the second measurement given for each one, again including the 2 cm tip, group them together and using 28-gauge wire bind firmly on the marks. Finally, wire and tape the 18-gauge wires together above the roots to make the trunk. (See Figs A, B and C.)

Building up the trunk

When the crown of the tree and the roots are completed, overlap the spare wires from each part, clipping them to make the tree a suitable

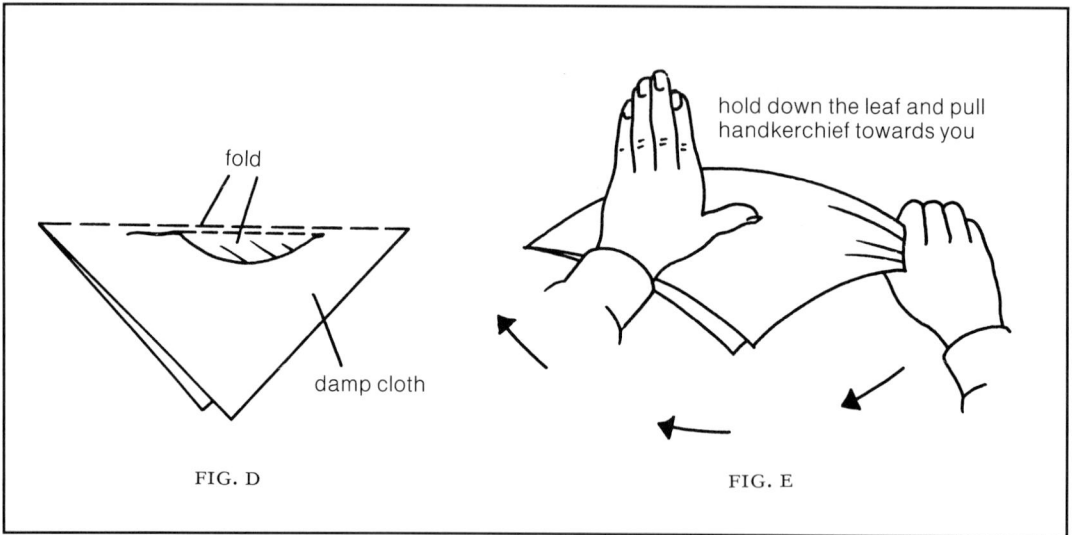

fold

damp cloth

FIG. D

hold down the leaf and pull handkerchief towards you

FIG. E

height, bearing in mind any curves that you may wish to make. Bind these two together very firmly all the way up with 28-gauge wire and cover in stem tape.

If the trunk requires extra thickness at this stage, first build it up to a uniform width with tissue and stem tape, then use kitchen foil crumpled around the trunk. This gives bulk without weight and can be moulded into a gnarled effect. Extra lumps can be made with smaller pieces of tightly crumpled foil under the first layer. Bind first with stem tape, to hold the foil in place (it does not need to cover it completely), then wrap with bonsai tape using half- or full-width depending on the bulk of the trunk.

An alternative method of making roots and trunk is to use a block of dry oasis. This is particularly useful in the cascade styles, which require a deep container, or a tree that has an extra thick trunk. First cut the oasis block to a conical shape with a flat top, $1\frac{1}{2}$ times the height of the pot. Secure it in the base of the pot at the correct angle with a prong. Plaster may be added to give weight to the base.

Complete the crown of the tree and thicken to the required length, and push the spare wires from the branches into the top of the cone as far as possible. The oasis can then be carved to shape and bound with bonsai tape.

Make small hairpins with 24-gauge wire to hold the tape down into the hollows. Texture to complete the bonsai.

Methods of texturing
Leaves and petals can be textured in two ways:

1 Take the leaf or petal and, holding between the first finger and thumb of each hand, twist as if twisting a toffee paper. Just half a turn will give a light texturing and twisting once or twice before unrolling will give a heavier texturing. Smooth the leaf to shape.
2 (Handkerchief texturing). Dampen a large cotton handkerchief (not wet). Place diagonally on the table and put the leaf or petal folded along its length in the centre. Fold the top of the handkerchief over so that the fold of the leaf is directly inside the fold of the handkerchief. Hold down the leaf with the heel of one hand and gather the corner of the handkerchief with the other. Pull it towards you and round through 180 degrees letting the leaf and handkerchief slide out from medium pressure in the last 60 degrees. Whether you are right or left handed, always remember to pull the leaf or petal from the top. (See Figs D and E.)

Texturing the trunk requires a little patience, and needs some acquaintance with the various sorts of bark. It is well worth while taking a walk in the local park or woods to look at the way bark grows on different trees.

The best way to simulate bark is to tear off short lengths of wide bonsai tape and glue them onto the trunk lengthways. If you pinch and mould the tape as it is applied, some interesting effects can be obtained. Feathering the edges, by tearing tiny pieces off, will help to disguise the straight edge on smooth bark. On rougher barks the edges can be pinched in. Very thick wallpaper paste can be used instead of glue, but leave the trunk to dry thoroughly before handling it.

'Cracks' that expose the bare trunk of the tree are allowable and all add to the aged look of the tree. To form a crack, lift the edges of the wet bonsai tape away from the trunk and insert a strip of lighter coloured tape underneath, and let the edges of the bark stand up as if they are peeling off.

Planting the tree

As mentioned in the previous chapter, the choice of pot is important. Try your bonsai in a selection of containers to see which will complement it the most for both colour and shape.

The position of the bonsai in the container is equally important. For example, in the case of a slanting style, the strongest roots should be at the side of the pot opposite the incline of the trunk to give a balanced effect. In an oblong or oval dish the tree looks best planted one-third of the way along. In a round or square dish try your bonsai off-centre for the best effect.

When container and position have been decided upon, take a piece of Dry Hard florist's clay, make it into a ball and press it firmly into the pot. If this will not adhere to the pot, try a piece of oasis fix or Blu-tack underneath the clay. Sit the tree on top of the clay so that when viewed from table level, the base of the tree and top of the roots are clearly seen. Shape the roots around and into the clay, twisting and spreading them to suit the style of the tree. The clay will dry quite solid in a few hours so be sure that your bonsai is looking just the way you want it before leaving it. Polystyrene can be used instead of the clay. Cut it to fit the pot and press the roots into it, spreading them as before. This is quite suitable for a small tree, but I feel that the larger specimens need the extra weight of the clay to hold them.

Finishing off

Any space in the pot can now be filled up. An easy way is to press gravel into the clay and leave it to set there.

Another way is to mix some plaster of paris and fill the dish to about half-full. If the mixture is quite stiff an uneven surface can be made, and scraped up around the roots. When set, paint with brown matt paint, and while still wet sprinkle on cork bits from a model shop.

Yet another method is to mix two parts fine peat and one part glue size with a little hot water and spread this onto the surface of the plaster or clay, between and over part of the root system to give a soil-like texture. This peat mixture will shrink a little and crack as it dries, but gives an interesting effect as long as the plaster was painted first. Whatever method is used the 'soil' should be below the level of the rim of the dish, and heaped up to, but not completely covering, the roots.

To give a natural aged look to the bonsai, part of the trunk and roots can be sprinkled lightly with grey or brown modelling powder. If convenient this can be done while the trunk is still wet with the texturing. When this has dried, dab on glue and green modelling powder to simulate lichen. Use this in the joints of the branches, mainly up one side only of the trunk, around the base and soil area. Natural dried lichen or reindeer moss can be used to similar effect.

1 Willow (*height 25 cm*)

Chapter 3
Learning the art

WILLOW (*YANIGI*)
In the weeping style (*shidare-zukari*)

Materials

75 cm each Bensilky Nos. 44 and 56
Wires in gauge 18, 22 and 28, green-covered
Stem tape – olive green
Bonsai tape – grey (1 roll)
Wide double-sided tape + glue or paste
Texturing materials

Leaves

Make leaves using wide double-sided tape and 28 wire as follows:

For the smallest leaf, cut off 6 cm of No. 56 ribbon and line with double-sided tape.

Crease into 8 sections each 6 cm × 0.9 cm.

Remove backing from tape. Place a 10 cm piece of 28 wire down the centre of each section. Back with No. 44 ribbon.

Cut to shape as shown in Diagram 1.

Repeat with second and third sizes allowing an extra 1 cm of stem for each size.

Make   8 leaves 6 cm × 0.9 cm
        24 leaves 7.2 cm × 1 cm
        20 leaves 8 cm × 1.2 cm

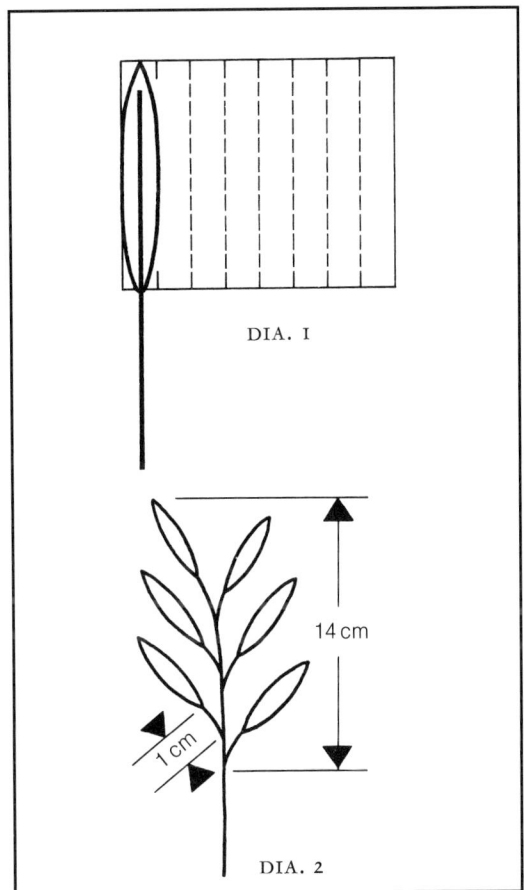

DIA. 1

14 cm

1 cm

DIA. 2

15

Texture leaves a little with the fingers and tape the stems with half-width olive tape. When making up the branches, allow 1 cm of leaf stem.

Branches

Cover half-pieces of 22 wire with stem tape and using quarter-width bonsai tape make up the branches as follows:

Branch A – make two. Example Diagram 2.
2 medium leaves + 4 large leaves = 14 cm.*

Branch B – make two.
2 medium leaves + 2 large leaves = 11 cm.*

Branch C – make four.
2 small leaves + 4 medium + 2 large leaves = 16.5 cm.* Thicken a little for further 3.5 cm, finish in bonsai tape.

Roots

Using basic methods and half-pieces of 18 wire make 5 roots in the following approximate sizes:

Double root – 10 cm × 0.5 cm
                     10 cm × 0.5 cm
Wire these two together 5 cm from the tips and treat as one root. Tape for 1 cm.

Single roots – 10 cm × 0.8 cm
                      10 cm × 0.9 cm
                      10 cm × 1 cm

Wire the roots together so that the double root measures 6 cm to the tips and the other roots measure 7 cm, 8 cm and 9 cm to their tips respectively.

Tape firmly above the join and clip the wires off 9 cm from the roots.

Assembling the tree (Diagrams 2a and 3)

Using quarter-width bonsai tape take one of branches A and B and join them together on a

*From the top of the first leaf to the base of the last leaf.

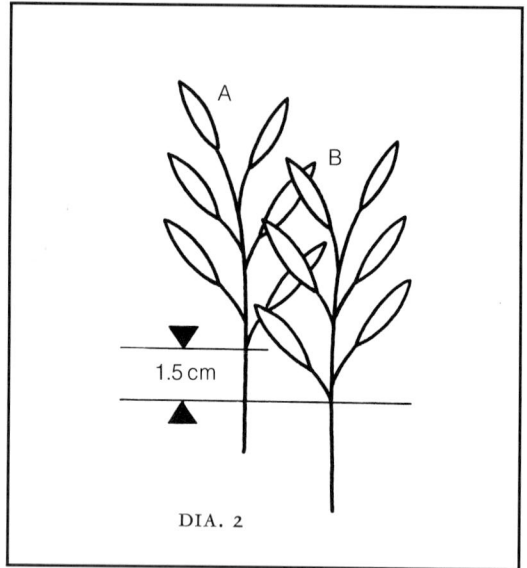

DIA. 2

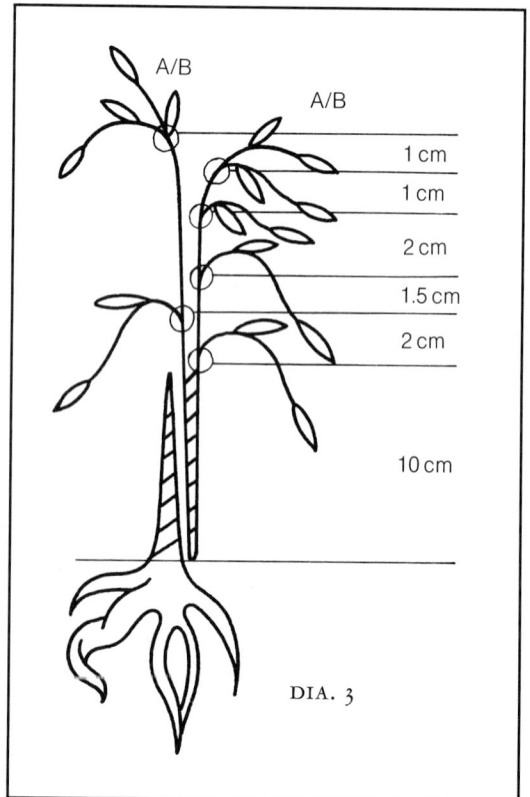

DIA. 3

half-piece of taped 18 wire 1.5 cm below the last leaf on A and level with the last leaf on B.

Repeat with second pair A and B.

Following measurements on Diagram 3 wire and tape these two pairs together.

Add first branch C 1 cm below to the left.

Add second branch C 2 cm below to right front, leaving 3 cm of branch to the lowest leaf. Thicken trunk a little proportionately and tape with half-width bonsai tape.

Add third branch C 1.5 cm below to left back, leaving 3.5 cm of branch to the lowest leaf. Thicken again.

Add fourth branch 2 cm below to right back, leaving 3.5 cm of branch.

Check position of branches by looking down from above. All the branches should be visible and not crossing one another.

Join the crown of the tree to the roots by overlapping the spare wires. Wire and tape firmly together.

The trunk should measure 10 cm from the lowest branch to the top of the roots.

Finishing touches

Thicken the trunk if necessary to 2 cm across at the base, tapering to 1 cm at the lowest branch.

Using short lengths of bonsai tape, texture as in basic methods, leaving the trunk with a fairly smooth appearance.

My container for this bonsai was made from one-half of the polystyrene packing round a travel clock, 8.5 cm square by 4 cm deep. I plastered it with polyfilla, keeping the texture deliberately rough, then painted it with matt paint. Matchpots are a good way of buying small amounts of emulsion paint for these jobs.

Plant the willow as described in basic methods. Fill up any space in the container with dried moss or gravel.

To give the tree an aged appearance, dab the trunk with glue and sprinkle lightly with grey modelling powder; then, using green powder to simulate lichen, apply over the roots, up one side of the trunk and in the branch joints.

The willow should measure 25 cm from the table top.

2 Cherry (*height 15 cm*)

CHERRY (FUJI-SAKURA)

Mame bonsai in the slanting style (*mame, shakan*)

Materials
25 cm Bensilky green No. 28
25 cm Bensilky green No. 5
3 Cherries (made or bought)
Wires in gauge 18 and 28 green
Stem tape – olive green
Bonsai tape – brown (1 roll)
5 mm double-sided tape + glue or paste
Texturing materials

Leaves
Cut off a piece of dark green ribbon 5 cm
× 7.2 cm. Crease it into four and stick a piece
of double-sided tape down the centre of each
section, as shown in Diagram 4.

Remove the backing and place a quarter-piece
of 28 wire on the double-sided tape; position
it a little down from the edge.

Place a piece of light green silky on top, and
seal the wires in by pressing with the fingers.

Cut into 4 sections along the creases, and
shape each leaf as shown in Diagram 4.

Texture each leaf by the damp handkerchief
method and tape the stems with half-width
stem tape.

Repeat until you have made 18 leaves.

Branches
Using half-pieces of 18 wire and quarter-
width bonsai tape, make up the branches to
the measurement given. Vary the length of
the leaf stem.

Branch A – Diagram 5.
Start with a taped bud on the wire end, add 2
leaves = 6 cm.

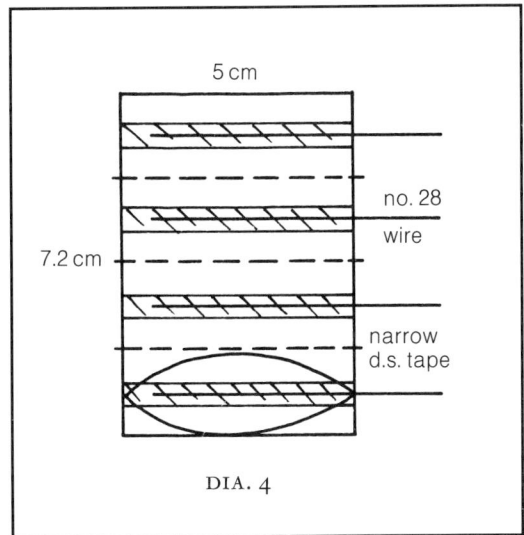

5 cm

7.2 cm

no. 28
wire

narrow
d.s. tape

DIA. 4

Branch B – Diagram 6.
Start with a taped bud and add 2 leaves; 1 cm
below add third leaf; 1 cm below that add two
more leaves = 8.5 cm. Thicken for a further
2.5 cm to 1 cm across, mark and taper off.

Branch C – Diagram 7.
Start with 2 leaves on an 18 wire; 2 cm below
add 3 cherries with a third leaf = 6.5 cm.
Thicken for 5 cm to 1.2 cm across, mark and
taper off.

Branch D – Diagram 8.
Tape together 3 leaves without an 18 wire.

5 leaves should be left

Using short lengths of bonsai tape, texture the
branches as described in the basic techniques.

Do not clip off the excess wires yet as these
will help to form the trunk.

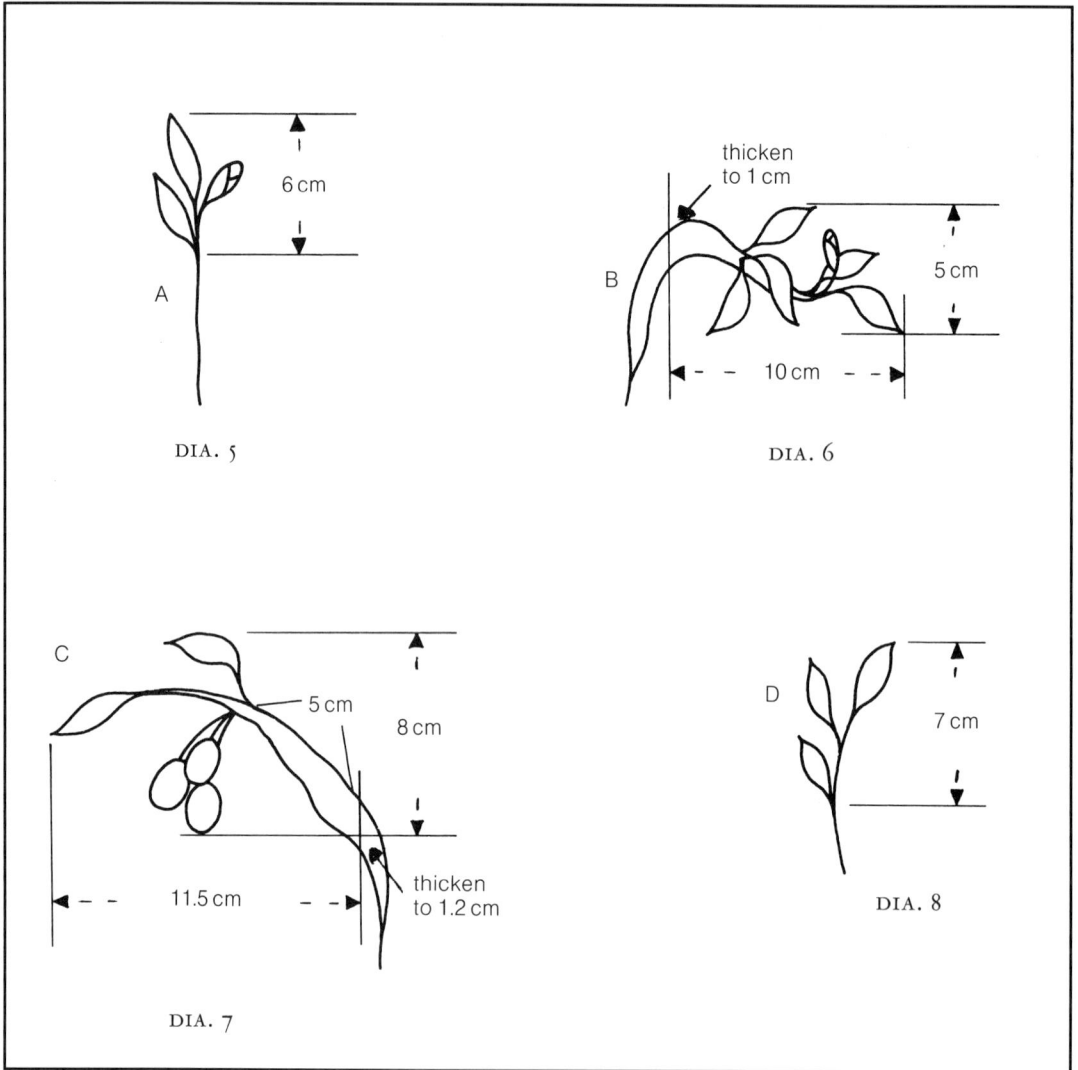

A 6 cm DIA. 5

B thicken to 1 cm 5 cm 10 cm DIA. 6

C 5 cm 8 cm 11.5 cm thicken to 1.2 cm DIA. 7

D 7 cm DIA. 8

Roots

Following the basic techniques and using half-pieces of 18 wire make 4 roots in these approximate sizes:

Double root – 8 cm × 0.8 cm
 8 cm × 1 cm

Wire these two together 6 cm and 7 cm from the tips, and treat as one root. Tape for 2 cm.

Single roots – 10 cm × 0.8 cm
 10 cm × 1 cm

Wire the roots together so that the double root measures 9 cm to the longest tip and the other two 8 cm and 8.5 cm to their tips respectively.

Tape firmly above the join and clip the wires off 11 cm from the roots.

Assembling the tree (Diagrams 9 and 10)
Tape branch A to the trunk, placing the lowest leaf directly at the top of the trunk wire.

Add a third leaf 0.5 cm down on the left.

Add a pair of leaves 1 cm lower on the right, and a second pair 0.5 cm below them on the left. Thicken a little as you go.

Camelia, Chinese Rose, White Pine, Red Maple (*Mame Bonsai*).

Apple Tree, (**top**) Japanese Apricot, (**bottom**) Scots
Pine, Rhododendron.

Now bend the roots so that the trunk leans to the right. Make sure that there is a strong root on the opposite side to the incline to balance the style.

8 cm from the bud top on branch A, bend the trunk backwards a little.

Build up the trunk to 1.8 cm across at the bend. The top of the tree can be textured at this stage if desired.

At the bend add branch B to the right and a little forward, wire and tape firmly. Wire D in behind the bend.

Continue to thicken the trunk proportionately and add branch C to the left, 3.5 cm below B.

Build up the trunk with foil if necessary to 3 cm across at the base. Wrap with bonsai tape and texture as in basic methods.

Finishing touches
Plant the bonsai as described in basic techniques. The dish I have used is a sweet little bonsai dish made by a local potter and obtained through a nearby bonsai society.

When planted the tree should measure no more than 15 cm from the table top. If the tree is too tall, bend the trunk a little more to comply with the mame style.

Fill the dish with peat mixture and dried moss. Dab glue on the trunk and roots and sprinkle with lichen-coloured texturing powder.

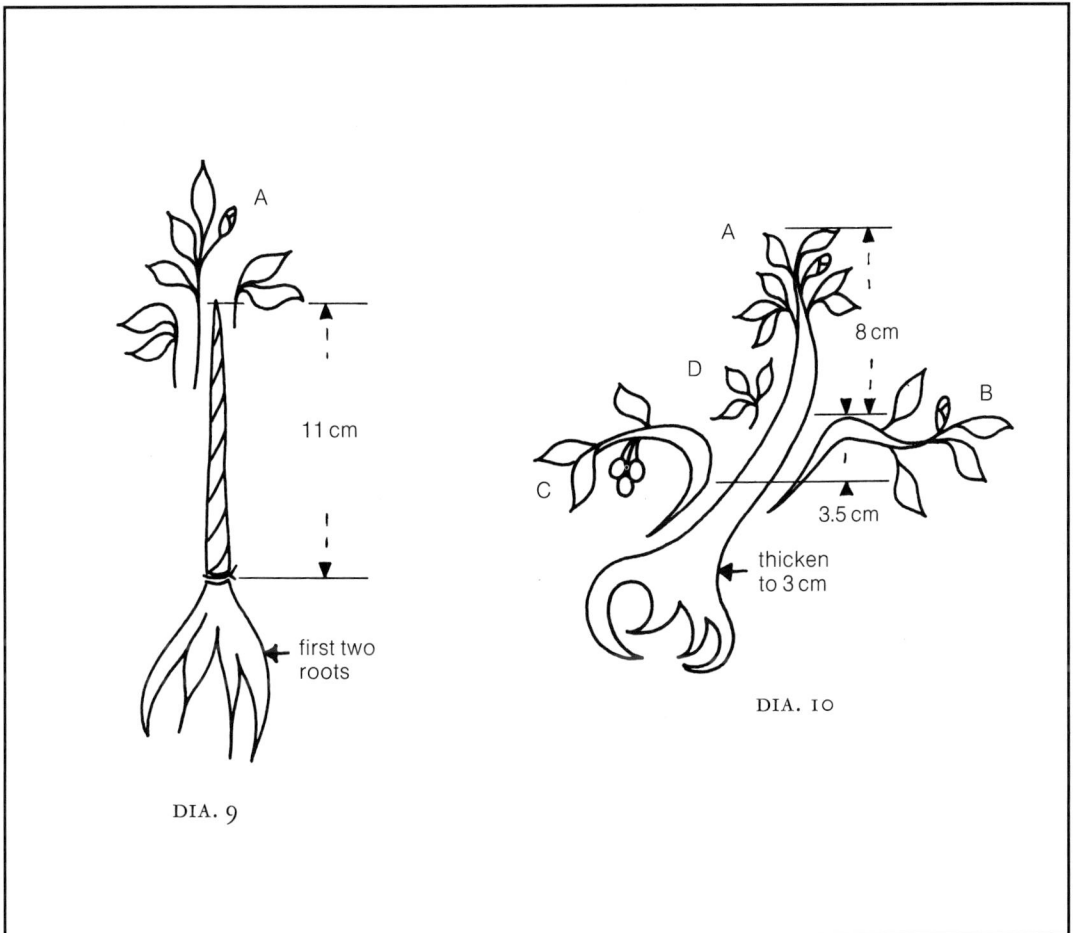

A

11 cm

first two roots

DIA. 9

A

8 cm

D

B

C

3.5 cm

thicken to 3 cm

DIA. 10

3 Red Maple (*height 13 cm*)

JAPANESE RED MAPLE (*MOMIJI*)
Informal upright, mame style (*Myogi-mame*)

Materials
50 cm Bensilky No. 17
Wires in gauges 18, 30 and 28 white
Stem tape – wine
Bonsai tape – brown ($\frac{1}{2}$ roll)
Wide double-sided tape + glue or paste
Texturing materials

Leaves
Line 3.6 cm squares of silky with double-sided tape, place a quarter-piece of 28 wire for the stem diagonally, and 2 small pieces of 30 wire as shown.

Back with a second square of ribbon and cut to shape as in Diagram 11.

Tape the stems with wine stem tape, vein with a pointed tool and finger texture lightly.

Make 12 leaves altogether.

Branches
Using quarter width bonsai tape make the leaves up into groups. Vary the length of leaf stem from 2 cm to 3 cm.

1 group with 4 leaves = 9 cm	from tip to last joint.	
2 groups with 3 leaves = 7 cm		
1 group with 2 leaves = 6 cm		

Thicken each leaf unit for 1 cm below the last leaf joint.

Roots
Make 3 roots on half-pieces of 18 wire as follows:

7 cm × 0.5 cm	Wire together	4 cm	to the
7 cm × 0.7 cm	so that roots	5 cm	tips
7 cm × 0.9 cm	are	6 cm	respectively

Clip wires off 12 cm above the roots, thicken to 1.5 cm across at the base of the trunk,

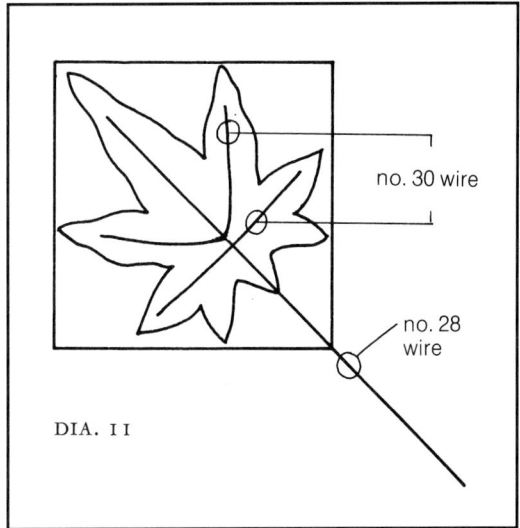

DIA. 11

no. 30 wire

no. 28 wire

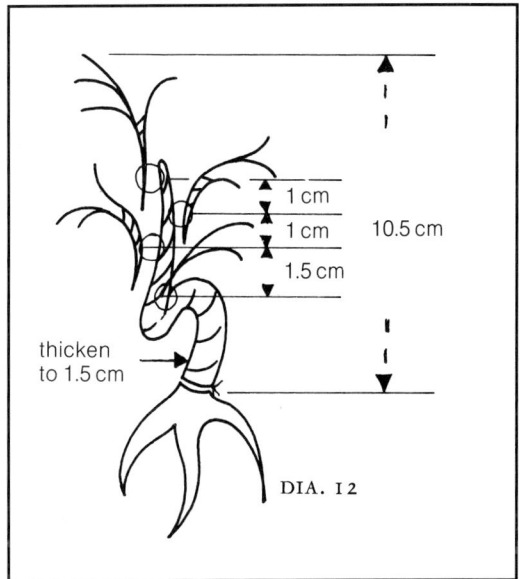

1 cm
1 cm
1.5 cm
10.5 cm

thicken to 1.5 cm

DIA. 12

tapering off to nothing at the top. Finish in bonsai tape.

Assembling the tree (Diagram 12)
Using half-width bonsai tape, join the 4-leaf unit directly onto the top of the trunk.

Add the 3-leaf unit, 1 cm below on the right.

Add the second 3-leaf unit 1 cm below on the left and a little to the front.

Bend the trunk to shape giving it a corkscrew effect, join in and bring the last 2-leaf unit over to the right.

Finishing touches

Texture the trunk with bonsai tape as in basic techniques.

I planted my tree in a tiny Japanese dish finished in a lovely metallic plum glaze. The colour complemented the colour of the leaves perfectly.

A small butter pot from a catering shop would also be suitable.

Fill up the dish with peat mixture and glue lichen-coloured modelling powder over the roots and trunk to age the tree.

The maple is about 13 cm high from the table top.

SCOTS PINE (*MATSU*)
Formal upright style (*chokkan*)

Materials

Wires in gauges 18, 22 and 28 green
Stem tape – beige
Bonsai tape – brown ($\frac{1}{2}$ roll)
Glue or paste
Texturing materials

Pine needle units

Cut 28-gauge green-covered wire into 6 cm pieces and bend each piece in half = 1 pair.

Make a small bud with beige tape on the end of a 10 cm piece of 22 wire, tape down to the end.

Using quarter-width bonsai tape, tape the pairs of pine needles around the bud end, work down the stem by placing each pair a fraction lower each time.

Use 8 to 12 pairs on each unit. The units should measure between 4 cm and 6 cm. Tape down to the end of the wire and spread the needles out a little (Diagram 13).

Make 21 units altogether.

Branches

Tape a half-piece of 18 wire with stem tape, then using quarter-width bonsai tape, tape on the pine needle units to the following measurements.

Allow 1.5 cm to 3.5 cm of stem on each unit when making up the branches.

Branch A
3 units = 7 cm.* Thicken the branch a little for 2.5 cm and mark.

Tape together 3 pairs of units. In each pair, 1 unit should be positioned a little higher than the other.

Add these 3 pairs to branch A where marked, each with a stem of 1 cm to 1.5 cm.

Branch B
5 units = 9 cm*

Branch C
7 units = 12 cm.*

Thicken B and C proportionately for a further 1.5 cm on each, to end up 0.8 cm across; mark and taper off.

Make 2 jinned (dead) branches by thickening up one-third pieces of 18 wire to about 0.5 cm across:

Branch D
1 piece 4.5 cm and 1 piece 2.5 cm joined together

Branch E
1 piece 2.5 cm

*From top of first unit to joint of last unit.

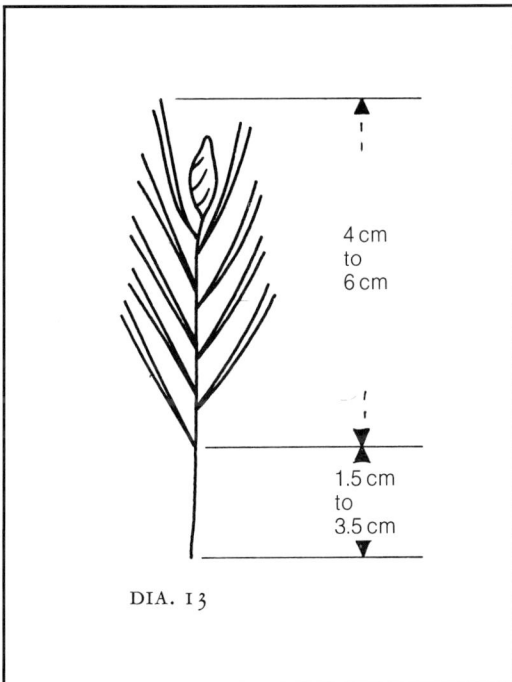

DIA. 13

Diagram labels: 4 cm to 6 cm; 1.5 cm to 3.5 cm

4 Scots Pine (*height 29 cm*)

Roots

Using basic methods, tape half-pieces of 18 wire and make 4 roots in the following sizes:

Double root – 2 roots 10 cm × 0.8 cm. Wire these two together 5 cm from the tips and treat as 1 root. Tape for 3 cm.

Single roots – 8 cm × 1 cm
          8 cm × 1.2 cm

Wire together so that the double root measures 8 cm to the tips and the other two are 6 cm and 6.5 cm to their tips respectively.

Tape firmly above the binding wire with stem tape.

Assembling the tree (Diagram 14)

Take the assembled branch A, wire and tape it to the root section so that the trunk measures 18 cm from branch A to the roots.

Bend the top 3 units of A over backwards.

From the top, thicken the trunk for 2.5 cm to 1 cm across and wrap with bonsai tape.

Wire and tape branch B to the left, and 1.5 cm lower add branch C to the right.

Thicken the trunk for 3.5 cm to 1.5 cm across and wrap with bonsai tape.

Wire jinned branch D to the right and slightly back, and 2 cm below that add branch E to the left back.

Check the position of the branches from above to make sure that they are not crossing over or hiding each other.

Thicken the trunk to 3.5 cm across at the base, tapering up to 2 cm at branches D and E.

Finishing touches

Plant the tree as in basic methods. I have chosen a dull round dish about 10 cm in diameter for this pine.

Texture the trunk with short lengths of bonsai tape as described in basic techniques. Try to achieve a scaled look by pushing the

tape up with the end of a pencil. While still wet, sprinkle all over with light-brown modelling powder.

Mix some peat mixture to fill up the dish, and add a few pebbles for interest. Dab with glue and press on some lichen-coloured powder over the root area, up one side of the trunk, and on the jinned branches.

The height of the pine is 29 cm from the table top.

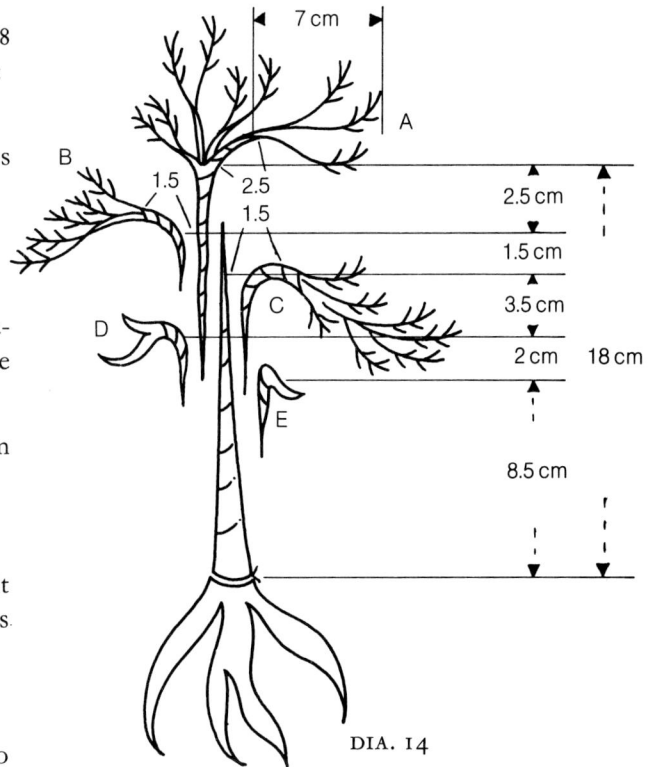

7 cm

A

B

1.5

2.5

1.5

D

C

E

2.5 cm

1.5 cm

3.5 cm

2 cm   18 cm

8.5 cm

DIA. 14

CHINESE ROSE (*BARA*)
Informal upright style (*myogi*)

Materials

75 cm Bensilky Ombre lemon No. 2
50 cm Roman Bensilky green No. 63
50 cm Bensilky green No. 28
2 cm Benlevy yellow
40 Stamens PT4
Wires in gauges 30, 18 and 26 lime green, 24 white and 28 (covered)
Stem tape – olive green and yellow
Bonsai tape – brown (1 roll)
Wide double-sided tape + glue or paste
Texturing materials

Flowers and buds

Petals for 2 flowers and 5 buds

Cut 9 petals from 7.2 cm squares as pattern in Diagram 15. Shape the petals by curling the top edge over a wire, and cupping the centre with the thumb. Alternatively flower irons may be used to shape the petals.

Centres for the flowers

Cut the velvet into 2 pieces each 1 cm × 7.2 cm. Fringe finely, and roll one of these around the hooked end of a piece of 24 wire. Secure with 30 wire and tape with yellow.

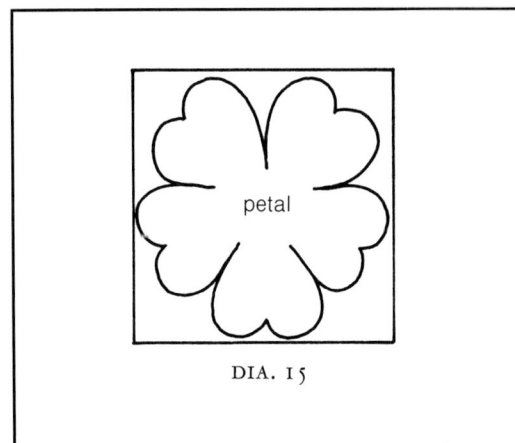

DIA. 15

Divide the stamens into 6 groups, wire and tape each group. Tape 3 groups around a velvet centre, spreading the stamens evenly.

Make a second centre in the same way.

Assembling the flowers

Make a hole in the centre of a petal and slide it up the stem to within 0.5 cm of the stamens, gather the petal in, twist wire and tape. The petal should curl outwards.

Make a cross-cut in the second petal and slide up the stem behind the first one. Just catch in the edges of the cross-cut with wire and tape. Do not gather this petal.

If using ombre ribbon position the colour on the opposite side to the first petal.

Tape on 5 green silk pointed sepals 2 cm × 0.3 cm – using olive tape.

Making the buds

Make a hook on the end of a piece of 24 wire and roll a piece of cotton wool into a ball around it.

Take a 3.6 cm square of yellow silk, place it over the cotton wool, gather it up underneath and twist wire. Tape in yellow.

Cut off 3 yellow sections from a petal, roll these 3 sections around the bud, curling inwards. Wire in place and tape in green. Tape on 5 silk sepals as for the flower.

Leaves

Using Roman silky No. 63, backed with plain silky No. 28, make 33 leaves 3.6 cm × 2.4 cm as follows:

Line the Roman with wide double-sided tape, place a quarter-piece of 26 wire as shown, back with the plain colour and cut to shape as in Diagram 16.

5 Chinese Rose (*height 23 cm*)

DIA. 16

DIA. 17

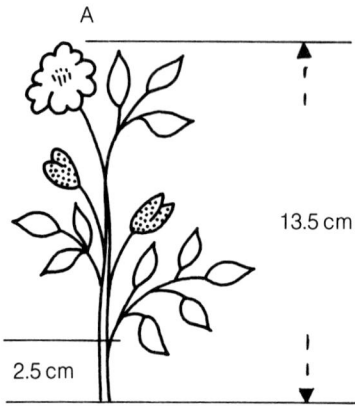

A

13.5 cm

2.5 cm

DIA. 18

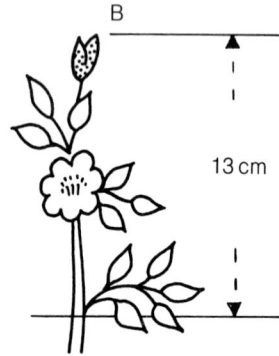

B

13 cm

DIA. 19

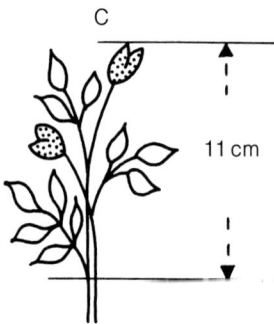

C

11 cm

DIA. 20

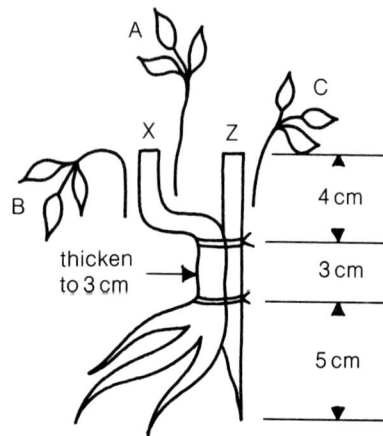

A

X   Z

C

4 cm

3 cm

5 cm

B

thicken
to 3 cm

DIA. 21

Tape the stems with half-width green tape, and mark veins with a pointed tool or flower iron.

Make up into 6 groups of 3 leaves, and 3 groups of 5 leaves, with about 1 cm of stem to each leaf as in Diagram 17.

Branches

Assemble as in the diagrams using quarter-width bonsai tape and adding half-piece of 18 wire at the first join.

Branch A – Diagram 18.
1 flower + 2 buds + 2 × 3 leaves + 1 × 5 leaves = 11 cm. Thicken slightly for a further 2.5 cm, finish in bonsai tape and mark.

Branch B – Diagram 19.
1 flower + 1 bud + 2 × 3 leaves + 1 × 5 leaves = 13 cm.

Branch C – Diagram 20.
2 buds + 2 × 3 leaves + 1 × 5 leaves = 11 cm.

Roots

Using basic methods make 3 roots on half-pieces of 18 wire in the following approximate sizes:

18 cm × 0.8 cm
18 cm × 1 cm
18 cm × 1.2 cm

Wire these three together 8 cm from the tips.

Tape firmly and clip off 10 cm above the binding wire, this will form stump X. Bend to shape as in Diagram 21.

Make a fourth root 12 cm × 1.5 cm and join to the others 5 cm from its tip. This will form stump Z.

Assembling the tree (Diagram 21)
Build up each stump if necessary to 1.5 cm across.

Using half-width bonsai tape, wire and tape branches A and B either side of stump X.

Wire and tape branch C on the right of stump Z.

Thicken the main trunk to 3 cm across and texture the trunk and stumps with short lengths of bonsai tape as in basic techniques.

Finishing touches
Plant the tree as described before. Place the trunk to one end of the rectangular container, which in this case is an inexpensive bonsai-style dish found in a seaside gift shop.

Fill any space in the dish with plaster and cover with dried moss to hide it.

Dab on glue and texturing powder if desired.

The rose should measure about 23 cm from the table top.

APPLE TREE (*KAIDO*)
Slanting style (*shakan*)

Materials

50 cm Bensilky green No. 41
50 cm Bensilky green No. 29
4 Apples (made or bought)
Wires in gauges 18 and 26 lime green, 28 (covered)
Stem tape – olive green
Bonsai tape – brown (1 roll)
Wide double-sided tape + glue or paste
Oasis cone and prong
Texturing materials

Leaves

Make 14 leaves from 3.6 cm squares, and 14 leaves from 3.2 cm squares as follows:

Line a piece of the darker green silky ribbon with wide double-sided tape, and place a quarter-piece of 26 wire as shown. Back with the light green silky and cut to shape as in Diagram 22.

Vein the leaves with a pointed tool or flower iron, and tape with half-width olive stem tape.

Branches

Using half-pieces of taped 18 wire and quarter-width bonsai tape, the leaves are joined on in a rosette form with about 1 cm of leaf stem.

Branch A – Diagram 23.

1. 0.5 cm down from the end of a piece of 18 wire, tape on 2 apples. Add 1 small and 2 large leaves around them. Thicken for 2 cm to 0.8 cm across, mark and taper off.

2. Start with a bud end on a piece of 18 wire. 2 cm from the end tape on 2 small leaves, and 1 cm below them add 3 large leaves. Thicken a little for 2 cm and mark.

Wire 1 and 2 together on the marks, thicken for 5.5 cm to 1 cm across, mark and taper off.

Branch B – Diagram 23.

0.5 cm from the end of a piece of 18 wire, tape on 1 apple and 2 small leaves. 0.5 cm below add 2 large leaves and 0.5 cm below them add 2 more large leaves. Thicken for 4 cm to 1 cm across, mark and taper.

Branch C – Diagram 24.

1. Make a bud end on a piece of 18 wire. 2 cm down from the end tape on 3 small leaves and 1 cm below add 2 large leaves. Thicken a little for 3 cm and mark.

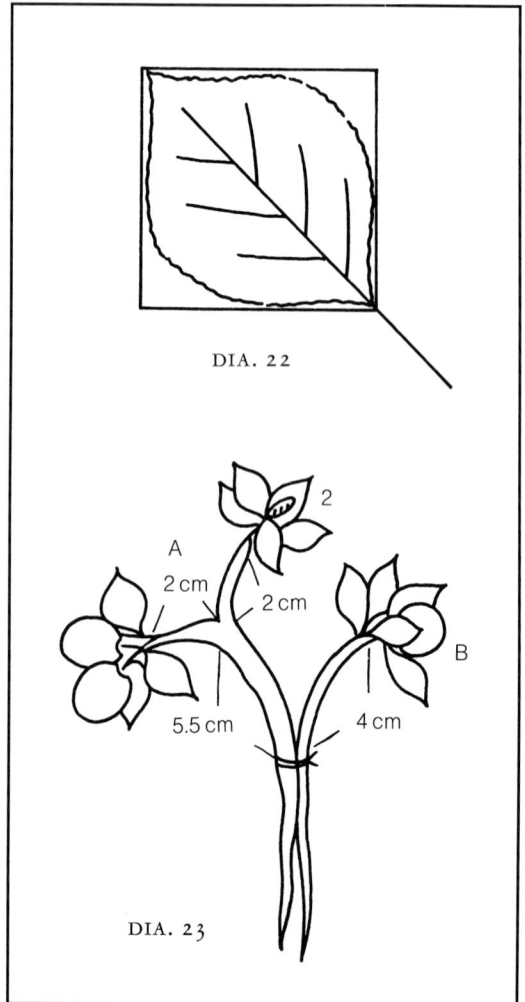

DIA. 22

DIA. 23

6 Apple (*height 25 cm*)

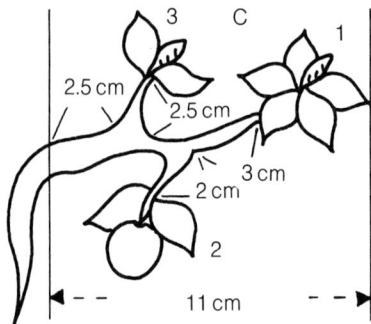

2.5 cm
2.5 cm
3 cm
2 cm
2
11 cm

DIA. 24

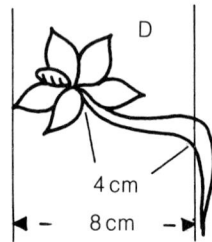

D
4 cm
8 cm

DIA. 25

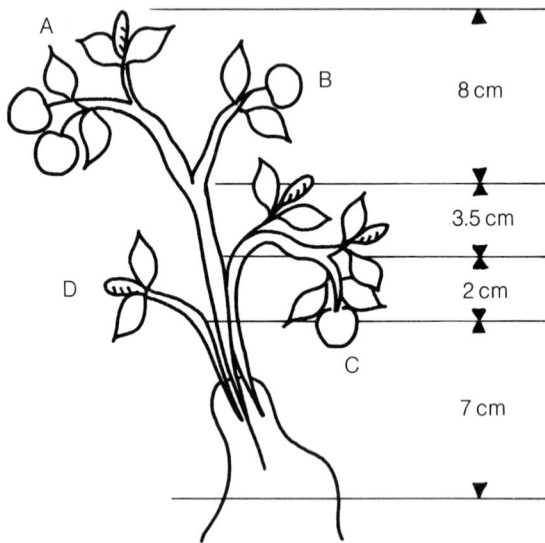

A
B
8 cm
3.5 cm
2 cm
D
7 cm
C

DIA. 26

2. 0.5 cm from the end of a piece of 18 wire, tape on 1 apple and 2 small leaves. Thicken a little for 2 cm and mark.

Wire 1 and 2 together on the marks and thicken for 2.5 cm to 0.8 cm across. Mark and taper.

3. Make a bud end on a piece of 18 wire and 2 cm from the end tape on 2 small leaves. Thicken for 2.5 cm to 0.8 cm across and mark.

Wire this section to 1 and 2 and thicken this branch for 2.5 cm to 1.3 cm across. Mark and taper off.

Branch D – Diagram 25.
Make a bud end on a piece of 18 wire. 2 cm from the end tape on 2 small leaves, and 1 cm below add 3 large leaves. Thicken for 4 cm to 1.3 cm across.

Roots
The root for this little apple tree is made from

a cone of dry oasis carved to shape.

I used an oblong dish made in pottery class for this one. Cut a small wedge shape off the base to make the cone slant to one side. Place the cone at one end of the dish and secure with a prong and oasis fix.

Shape the cone with a knife to take off the straight look.

Assembling the tree (Diagram 26)
Wire branches A and B together on the marks, and thicken for 3.5 cm to 1.5 cm across.

Add branch C to the right and towards the back. Thicken the trunk a little more and 2 cm below C add branch D to the left and towards the front.

Check the position of the branches from above.

Bind all the branch wires together and push into the top of the oasis cone at an angle.

Finishing touches
Build up the trunk with foil and stem tape, moulding it around the join and into the shape of the trunk.

The base of the tree should be about 5 cm across and the trunk should measure about 7 cm from branch D to the top of the dish.

Wrap the trunk with bonsai tape, pinning it into the shape of the trunk with small hairpins of wire.

Bend the branches to shape and texture with bonsai tape as in basic techniques.

Fill the dish half-full with plaster of paris and make up some peat mixture to cover it. I sprinkled a layer of cork granules over that.

Glue lichen-coloured powder around the base of the tree and on the trunk and branches to simulate moss.

The apple tree is about 25 cm high from the table top.

7 Rhododendron (*height 26 cm*)

RHODODENDRON (*SHAKUNAGE*)
Semi-cascade style (*hai-kengai*)

Materials

150 cm Bensilky Ombre cyclamen No. 26 or
Poplin Ombre No. 14 or 15.
150 cm Bensilky green No. 41
5 cm Bensilky green No. 29
150 cm Satin Acetate green No. 41
Stamens pink PT4
Wires in gauges 18, 30 and 26 pink; 24 and 28
green
Stem tape – nile green and moss green
Bonsai tape – brown (2 rolls)
5 mm double-sided tape
Wide double-sided tape + glue or paste
Texturing materials

Flowers and buds

Petals

Cut ombre silk into 9 pieces each 10.5 cm
× 7.2 cm for the flower, and 7 pieces each
7.2 cm × 7.2 cm for the bud.

Cut to shape as in Diagrams 27 and 28.

Curl and cup the tops of the petals or lightly
tool with a ridged foot in the direction of the
arrows.

Stick half-width of 5 mm double-sided tape

on the shaded area, form the petals into a cone
shape and stick together with the tips curling
outwards on the flowers and inwards on the
buds.

Centres and assembly of open florettes

First make the stigma. Take a quarter-piece of
pink 26 wire and make a small taped end in
nile green. Bend this over.

Cut one end off 9 stamens, and tape these
around the stigma so that it protrudes 1.5 cm
above the stamen heads.

Make a small hole in the bottom of the petal
cone and pass the stamen centre through so
that the stamen heads are level with the petal
separations.

Twist wire the base of the petal 1 cm up, and
tape with nile green.

Centres and assembly of florette buds

Make a ball of cotton wool on the end of one-
third of a piece of 26 wire. Make a small hole
in the base of a bud petal and pass the wire
through.

Dab a little glue around the petal tops and
draw together over the top of the cotton

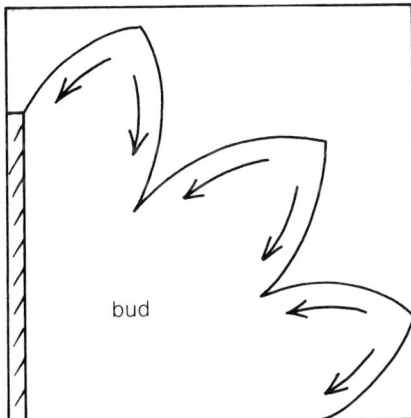

bud

DIA. 28

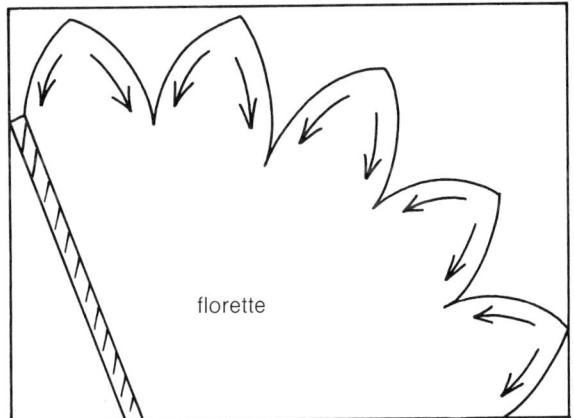

florette

DIA. 27

DIA. 29

DIA. 30

DIA. 31

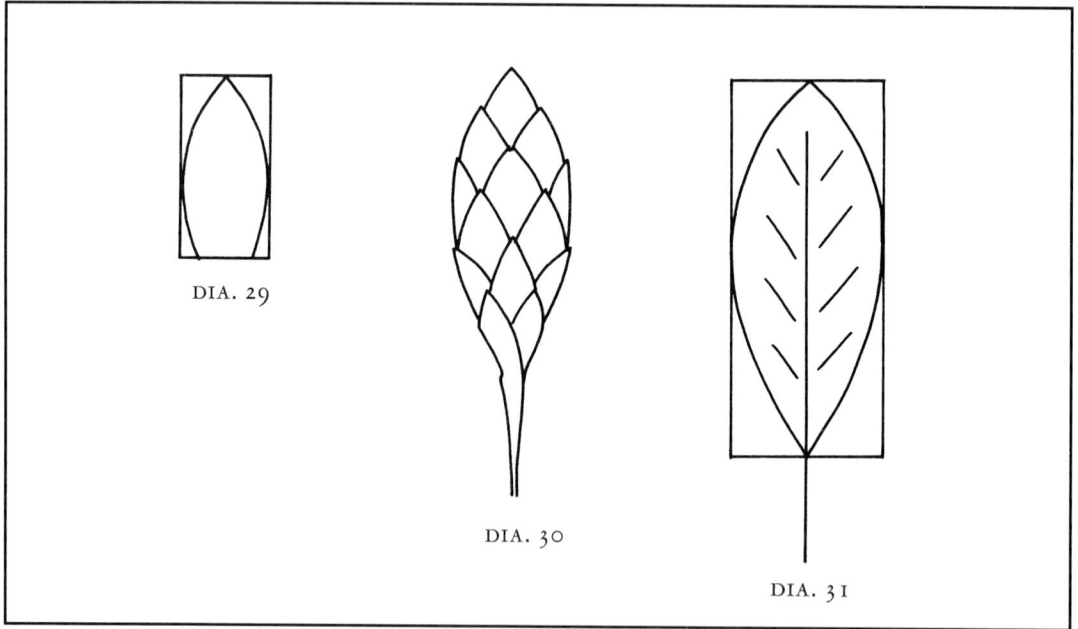

wool. Wire and tape the base as for the florettes.

Green bud

Cut green silky No. 29 into pieces 2.4 cm × 1.2 cm and cut to shape as in Diagram 29.

Thicken and tape the end of an 18 wire – 4 cm long × 1.5 cm at the widest point as in Diagram 30.

Glue silky pieces around the taped bud, overlapping them and working from the top to the base. Neaten with nile tape.

Leaves

Line the green satin with wide double-sided tape and cut into sections as follows:

Size 1 – 16 pieces 10 cm × 3.6 cm.
Size 2 – 10 pieces 9 cm × 3 cm.
Size 3 – 6 pieces 8 cm × 2.4 cm

Place half a piece of 24 wire down the centre of each section, back with green silky and cut to shape as in Diagram 31

Mark veins with a pointed tool or heated blade, and tape the stems in moss green.

Branches.
Branch A

Tape an 18 wire and using moss green, tape the 7 florette buds around the top.

Leaving between 1 cm and 2 cm of leaf stem add leaves as follows:

0.5 cm below, tape on 3 size 3 leaves.
0.5 cm below, tape on 3 size 2 leaves.
1 cm below, tape on 3 size 1 leaves.
1 cm below, tape on 3 more size 1 leaves.

Branch B

Take the wire with the green bud, add leaves:

1 cm below, tape on 3 size 3 leaves.
0.5 cm below, tape on 3 size 2 leaves.
0.5 cm below, tape on 5 size 1 leaves.

Thicken the branch for 8 cm to 1.2 cm across, mark and taper off.

Branch C

Tape an 18 wire and tape the 9 florettes around the top.

2 cm below, tape on 4 size 2 leaves.
1 cm below, tape on 3 size 1 leaves.
1 cm below, tape on 2 size 1 leaves.

Thicken the branch for 11 cm to 1.2 cm across, mark and taper off.

Roots

Using basic methods make 3 roots in sizes:

16 cm × 1.2 cm	Wire together	10 cm	to the
16 cm × 1.4 cm	so that roots	12 cm	tip
16 cm × 1.6 cm	are	15 cm	respectively

Tape together firmly above the join.

Assembling the tree (Diagram 32)

Wire and tape branch A to the top of the root section, overlapping the wires so that the trunk measures 35 cm from A to the top of the roots. Thicken for 13 cm to 1.2 cm across and wrap with bonsai tape.

Wire in branch B on the left and thicken for 8 cm to 2 cm across, wrap with bonsai tape.

Wire in branch C on the left and thicken to 3 cm across at the base of the trunk, wrap with bonsai tape.

Bend the trunk to shape, bringing C over the top of the main trunk to face right front.

Texture with short lengths of bonsai tape, and sprinkle with light brown texturing powder while still wet.

Finishing touches

Plant the tree as before in a deepish container. Mine was one from my friendly potter and was about 8 cm square and 6 cm deep.

The pot was half-filled with plaster to give weight, and after planting a layer of peat mixture was put on top and mounded up around the roots. Cover lightly with cork granules for interest.

Lichen-coloured modelling powder can be glued on the trunk here and there to simulate moss.

The height of the rhododendron is about 26 cm from the table top, but it should cascade over the edge of the pot to just touch or hang below the table edge.

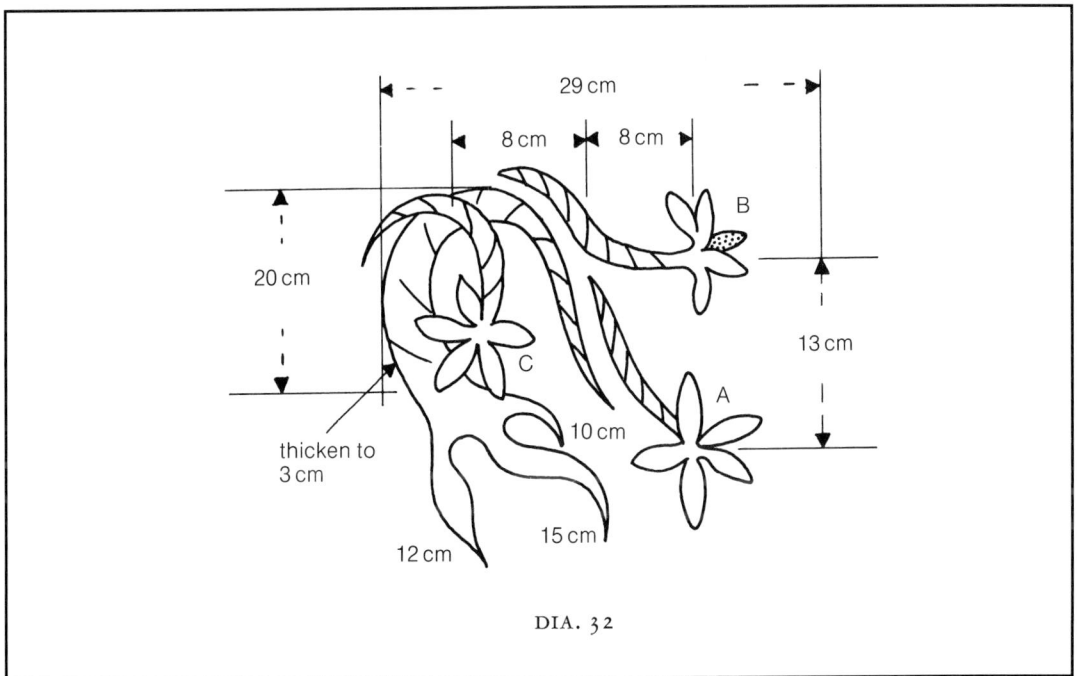

DIA. 32

8 Cotoneaster (*height 12.5 cm*)

COTONEASTER HORIZONTALIS
(BENI-SHITAN)
Mame bonsai in semi-cascade style
with exposed root system

Materials

25 cm Satin acetate green No. 28 or 41
25 cm Bensilky green No. 28
20 Cotoneaster berries
Wires in gauges 18, 22 and 28 green
Bonsai tape – brown ($\frac{1}{2}$ roll)
Wide double-sided tape + glue or paste
Texturing materials

Leaves

Line the satin with wide double-sided tape, mark the leaf sizes and place pieces of 28 wire with a 1.5 cm stem allowance in the centre of each section as shown.

Back with silky and cut to shape as in Diagram 33.

Make 12 leaves each 3 cm × 1.5 cm
18 leaves each 2.4 cm × 1.2 cm
28 leaves each 1.8 cm × 1 cm

Branches

Using half-pieces of taped 22 wire and quarter-width bonsai tape, make up the branches as in the Diagrams. Use the smallest leaves at the tops of the branches.

Branch A – Diagram 34.
14 leaves + 8 berries = 8 cm.

Branch B – Diagram 35.
31 leaves + 7 berries = 9.5 cm. Thicken for 2.5 cm to 0.6 cm across, mark and taper off.

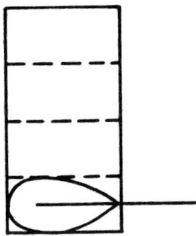

DIA. 33

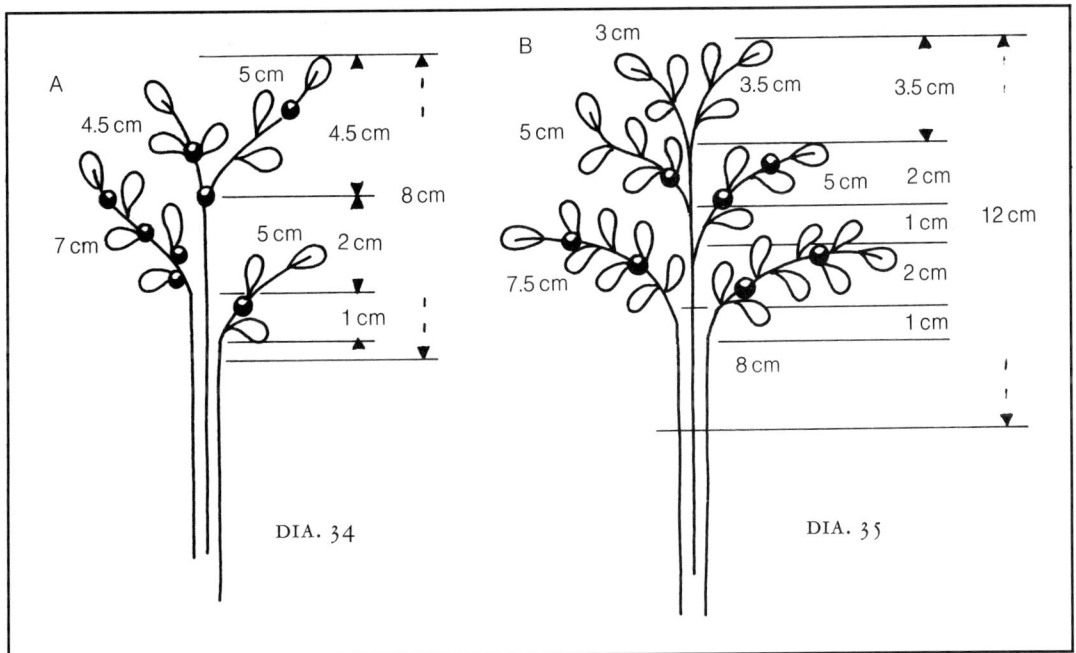

DIA. 34   DIA. 35

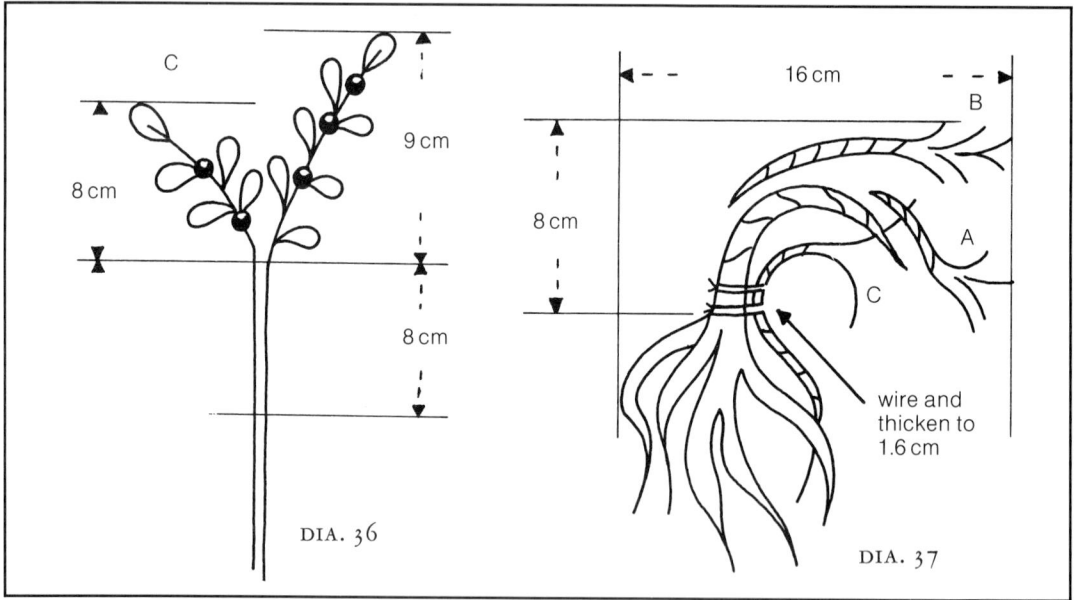

DIA. 36

DIA. 37

Branch C – Diagram 36.

12 leaves + 5 berries = 9 cm. Thicken for 8 cm to 0.7 cm across, mark and taper off.

Roots

Using basic techniques make 5 roots on half-pieces of 18 wire, thicken along the full length to between 0.4 cm and 0.8 cm across, finish in half-width bonsai tape.

To form the exposed root system, wire two of the thickest roots together half-way up and tape with bonsai tape.

Add a third root 2.5 cm above the join and tape again.

Add the 2 last and thinnest roots 1.5 cm above that. Tape all the wires above the last join firmly together.

Assembling the tree (Diagram 37)

Join branch A to the top of the root system, overlapping so that the top of the root wires come to the base of the lowest twig on branch A.

Thicken for 5.5 cm to 0.8 cm across and bend to shape.

Join in branch B at the top of the bend, trimming the wires to suit.

Join in branch C where the top of the root system begins, 2 cm below B, on the right side towards the front.

It is easier to leave the spare wires on C to form a sixth root, as long as the branch is bound in with wire and tape for about 1 cm to look like an integral part of the trunk. The trunk should be about 1.6 cm across at this point.

Finishing touches

Plant the bonsai as in basic techniques.

I used a small bonsai pot for this one about 6.5 cm deep. The roots are exposed for 4 cm above the rim of the pot before the tree cascades over the edge.

Fill up the pot with peat mixture covered with cork granules.

Brown texturing powder was used all over the branches and roots of this little bonsai instead of the usual texturing with tape. A little lichen-coloured powder was also sprinkled around the roots.

The cotoneaster stands about 12.5 cm from the table top to the highest point.

CAMELIA (*TSUBAKI*)
Informal upright style (*myogi*)

Materials

25 cm Bensilky in red or pink
2 cm Benlevy in yellow
4 cm Bensilky in white
30 cm Satin acetate in green No. 28 or 41
50 cm Bensilky green No. 29
Wires in gauges 30, 20, 18, 24 and 28 green
Stem tape – nile green
Bonsai tape – grey (1 roll)
Wide double-sided tape + glue or paste
Texturing materials

Flowers and buds

Petals for 1 flower and 2 buds
Cut 11 petals as pattern from 3.6 cm squares (Diagram 38).

Shape the petals by pulling the top edge over your scissors to curl, and cupping the centre with your thumb. Alternatively flower irons may be used to shape the petals.

Centres for the flowers
Cut the velvet into 2 pieces, each 1 cm × 7.2 cm, fringe these finely and roll one of them around the taped end of one-third of a piece of 20 wire. Secure with 30 wire and neaten with stem tape.

Cut the white silky ribbon into two pieces, each 2 cm × 7.2 cm, fringe finely and colour the tip of the fringe with yellow felt pen. Roll one of these around the yellow velvet, secure and neaten as before – curl inwards.

Make two more centres for the buds, in each case using half the length of the remaining pieces.

Assembling the flower and buds
Wire up 5 petals in single sequence. Wrap the petals around the centre to just overlap. Secure the wire and tape with half-width stem

tape. The petals should curl outwards.

Alternatively, place the petals evenly around the centre and secure with 30 wire.

Open up the flower slightly.

Make the flower buds in the same way using 3 petals on each. Leave in a closed position.

For the calyx, cut 11 pieces of green silky 2.4 cm × 1.2 cm to shape as in Diagram 39.

Glue 5 pieces around the base of the flower, and 3 pieces around each of the buds, round side up, to form the calyx. Neaten with tape.

Green buds
Make a small hook on the end of a 6 cm piece of 24 wire, thicken the end with tissue and tape to form one fat bud about 2 cm long × 1 cm across. Make 11 smaller buds, varying the sizes down to 1 cm × 0.4 cm.

DIA. 39 calyx

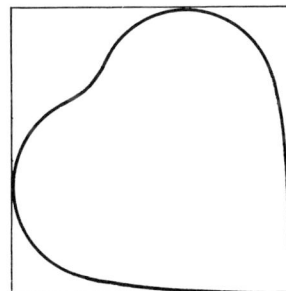

DIA. 38 petal

9 Camelia (*height 25 cm*)

Willow, Red Maple (*Mame*), Japanese Mountain
Maple, Fruiting Cherry (*Mame*).

Chinese Tulip Tree, Flowering Cherry, (***top***)
Cotoneaster Horizontalis, (*Mame*) (***bottom***) English
Oak.

DIA. 40 bud

DIA. 41 leaves

make up the branches as in the diagrams.

Build up the thickness towards the lower end with extra tissue and stem tape, mark and taper off. Use bonsai tape for the final layer.

Branch A – Diagram 42.
1 flower bud + 1 large and 2 smaller green buds + 4 leaves = 8.5 cm.* Thicken for a further 3.5 cm to 0.5 cm across.

Branch B – Diagram 43.
1 flower + 3 green buds + 4 leaves = 11 cm.* Thicken for a further 2.5 cm to 0.8 cm across.

Branch C – Diagram 44.
1 green bud + 2 leaves = 7 cm.*

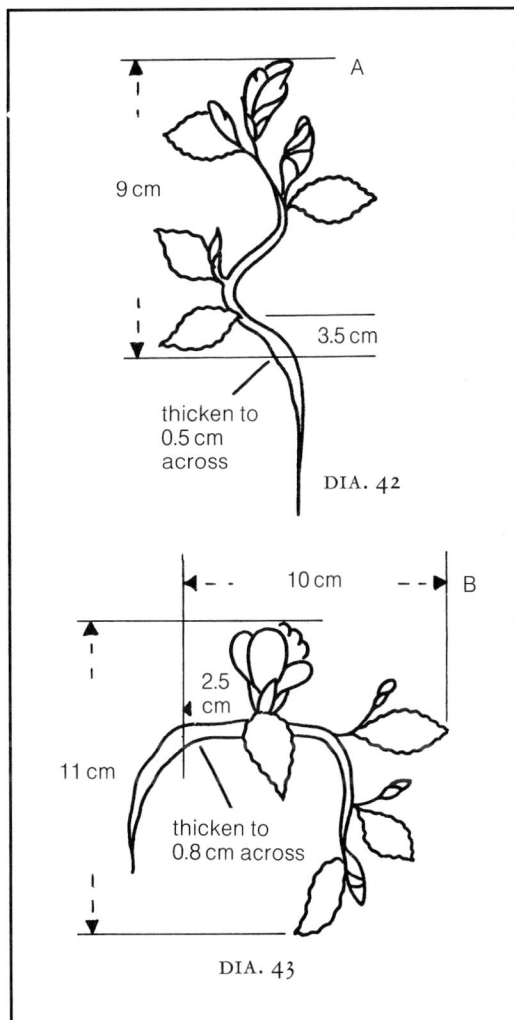

9 cm

3.5 cm

thicken to
0.5 cm
across

DIA. 42

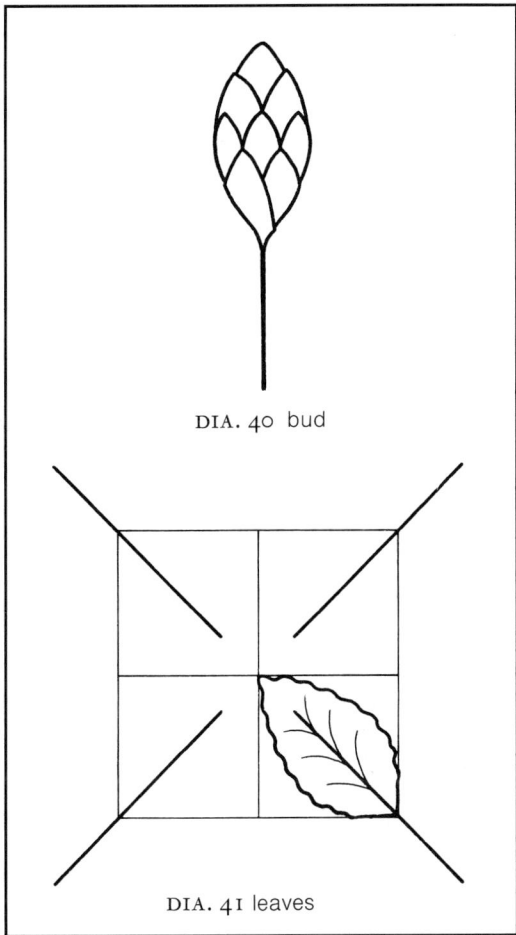

Cut green silky into pieces 1.2 cm × 0.9 cm the same shape as before, and glue onto the green taped buds, round side up and overlapping them as in Diagram 40. Neaten with tape.

Leaves
To make 4 leaves line a piece of green satin 7.2 cm square with wide double-sided tape, crease into 4 sections. Place 9 cm pieces of 24 wire diagonally across each section as shown in Diagram 41, back with green silky and cut to shape. Mark the veins with a pointed tool or flower iron. Tape all the stems with half-width stem tape.

Make 14 leaves in all.

Branches
Using 18 wire and quarter-width bonsai tape,

10 cm   B

2.5
cm

11 cm

thicken to
0.8 cm across

DIA. 43

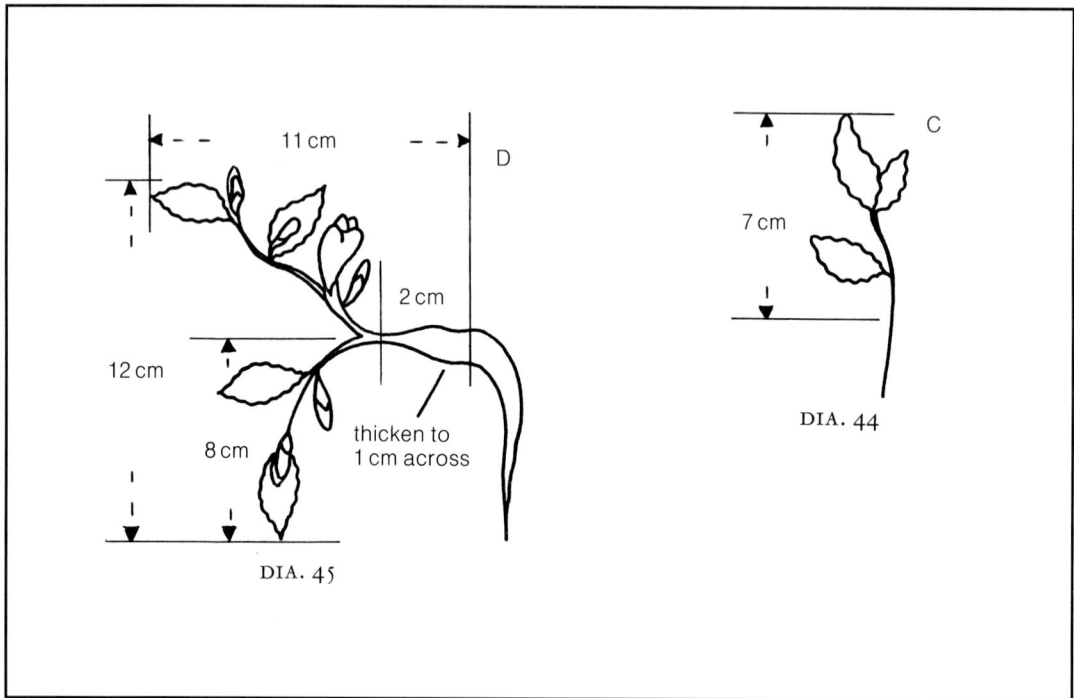

11 cm

D

2 cm

12 cm

8 cm

thicken to
1 cm across

DIA. 45

C

7 cm

DIA. 44

Branch D – Diagram 45.
1 flower bud+5 green buds+4 leaves =
11 cm.* Thicken for further 2 cm to 1 cm
across.

*When extended from tip of first leaf to base of last leaf.

Do not clip off spare wires yet as these will
help to form the trunk.

Roots
Using basic methods make 5 roots on half-
pieces of 18 wire in the following approximate sizes.

10 cm × 0.5 cm	Wire together	5.5
10 cm × 0.8 cm	so that roots	6 cm
10 cm × 1 cm	are	6 cm	to tips
10 cm × 1 cm		6.5 cm	respectively.
10 cm × 1.2 cm		7.5 cm

Tape all 5 together firmly above the binding
wire to form the trunk.

Clip all the wires off about 13 cm from the
roots.

Assembling the tree (Diagram 46)
Wire branches A and B together, 3.5 cm
below last leaf on A and 2.5 cm below flower
on B.

Overlap the wire below the join with the main
trunk wires from the roots. Position the
thickest root on the right. Clip off any surplus
wire near the base of the tree, wire and tape
firmly together.

Build up the trunk to about 2.5 cm across for
the first 5 cm from the base. Add in branch D
at about that point, on left and slightly
forward.

Taper the rest of the trunk up to A/B adding
branch C towards the back about 2.5 cm
below the junction of A and B.

Finishing touches
When everything is firm and in proportion,
bind with bonsai tape and bend the trunk with
pliers to a suitable shape so that the tree is no
more than 22 cm high (roots excluded).

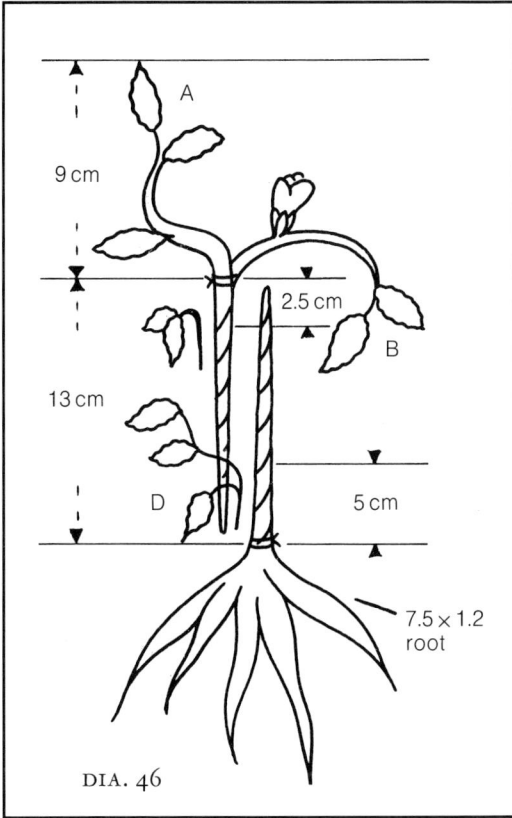

9 cm

2.5 cm

A

B

13 cm

D

5 cm

7.5 × 1.2
root

DIA. 46

Plant the camelia as described in the chapter on basic techniques. The position of the tree in the dish is important. I used a small rectangular dish made in pottery class, and planted my tree towards one end to balance the informal curve of the trunk.

Short lengths of bonsai tape may now be pasted on to give a bark-like texture, as described in basic techniques. Allow to dry thoroughly.

The camelia can be aged by dabbing glue around the base, on the exposed roots and mainly on one side of the trunk. Press green-coloured modelling powder onto the glue to give the effect of lichen.

Fine gravel or pretty pebbles can be used to fill up the dish and disguise the clay.

The tree should measure about 25 cm from the table top.

10 English Oak (*height 33 cm*)

ENGLISH OAK (*KASHIWA*)
Formal upright style (*chokkan*)

Materials
125 cm Roman Bensilky No. 63
125 cm Bensilky green No. 29
8 Acorns (made or bought)
Wires in gauges 18, 26 fawn and 28 (covered)
Stem tape – brown
Bonsai tape – brown (1 roll)
Wide double-sided tape + glue or paste
Texturing materials

Leaves
Mark off 8 sections, each 7.2 cm × 3.6 cm on the roman silky. Cut off in one piece and back with double-sided tape.

Place a quarter-piece of 26 wire down the centre of each section, with the stem to the dark edge. Back with the plain silky, and cut into sections, as shown. Cut each section into an oak leaf shape as in Diagrams 47 and 48.

Tape the stems with half-width stem tape, and mark veins with a pointed tool or flower iron.

Repeat the instructions above, making 14 medium leaves 6 cm × 3 cm, and 18 small leaves 5 cm × 2.5 cm. In each case cut off some of the dark edge to get the longest measurement correct, and be sure to place the stems to the darkest edge.

Branches
Using half-pieces of 18 wire and quarter-width bonsai tape, make small branches as shown in example A, Diagram 49.

Add an 18 wire with the third leaf and thicken a little between each addition. Vary the length of the leaf stem.

Branch A
3 small leaves + 2 acorns = 8 cm.* Thicken proportionately for 2.5 cm to 1 cm across at the base, mark and taper off.

Branch B
3 small leaves = 8 cm.* Thicken for 1 cm to 0.8 cm across, mark and taper.

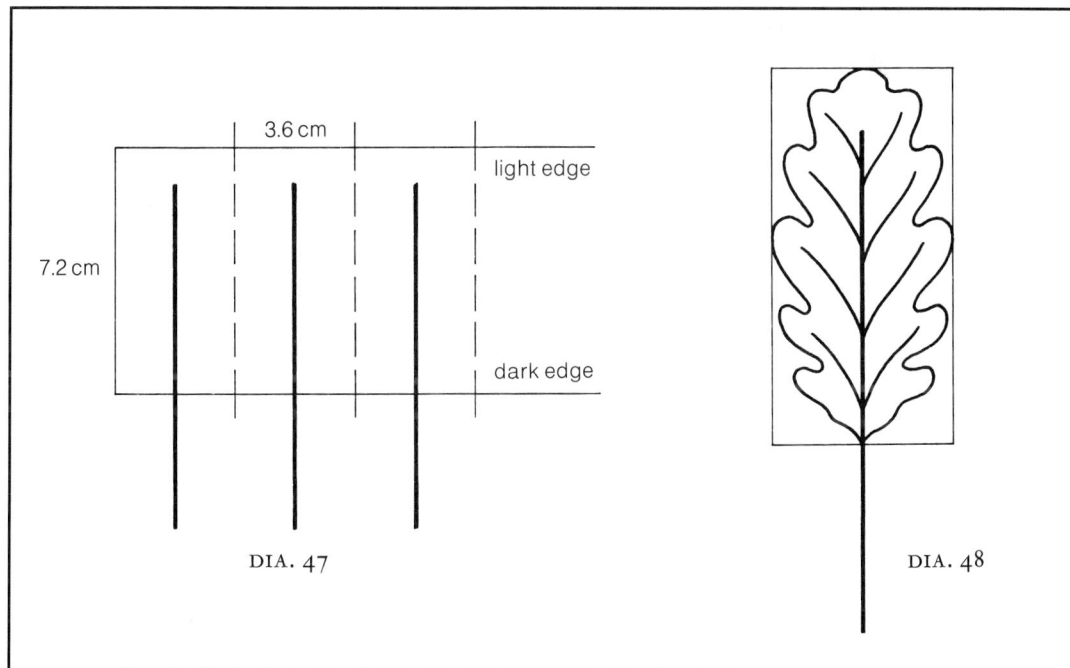

DIA. 47   DIA. 48

Branch C

2 small + 2 medium leaves = 9 cm.* Thicken for 2.5 cm to 1 cm across, mark and taper.

Branch D

2 small leaves + 1 acorn + 3 medium leaves = 11 cm.* Thicken for 0.8 cm to 0.5 cm across, mark and taper.

Branch E

1 medium leaf + 2 acorns + 2 large leaves = 10 cm.* Thicken for 1.5 cm to 0.8 cm across.

Branch F

2 small leaves + 1 acorn + 3 medium leaves = 9.5 cm.* Thicken for 3 cm to 1 cm across, mark and taper.

Join together E and F on the marks, binding with wire and tape. Thicken for 3 cm to 1 cm across, mark and taper off (Diagram 50).

Branch G

2 small + 2 medium leaves + 2 acorns + 1 large leaf = 10.5 cm.* Thicken for 2 cm to 1 cm

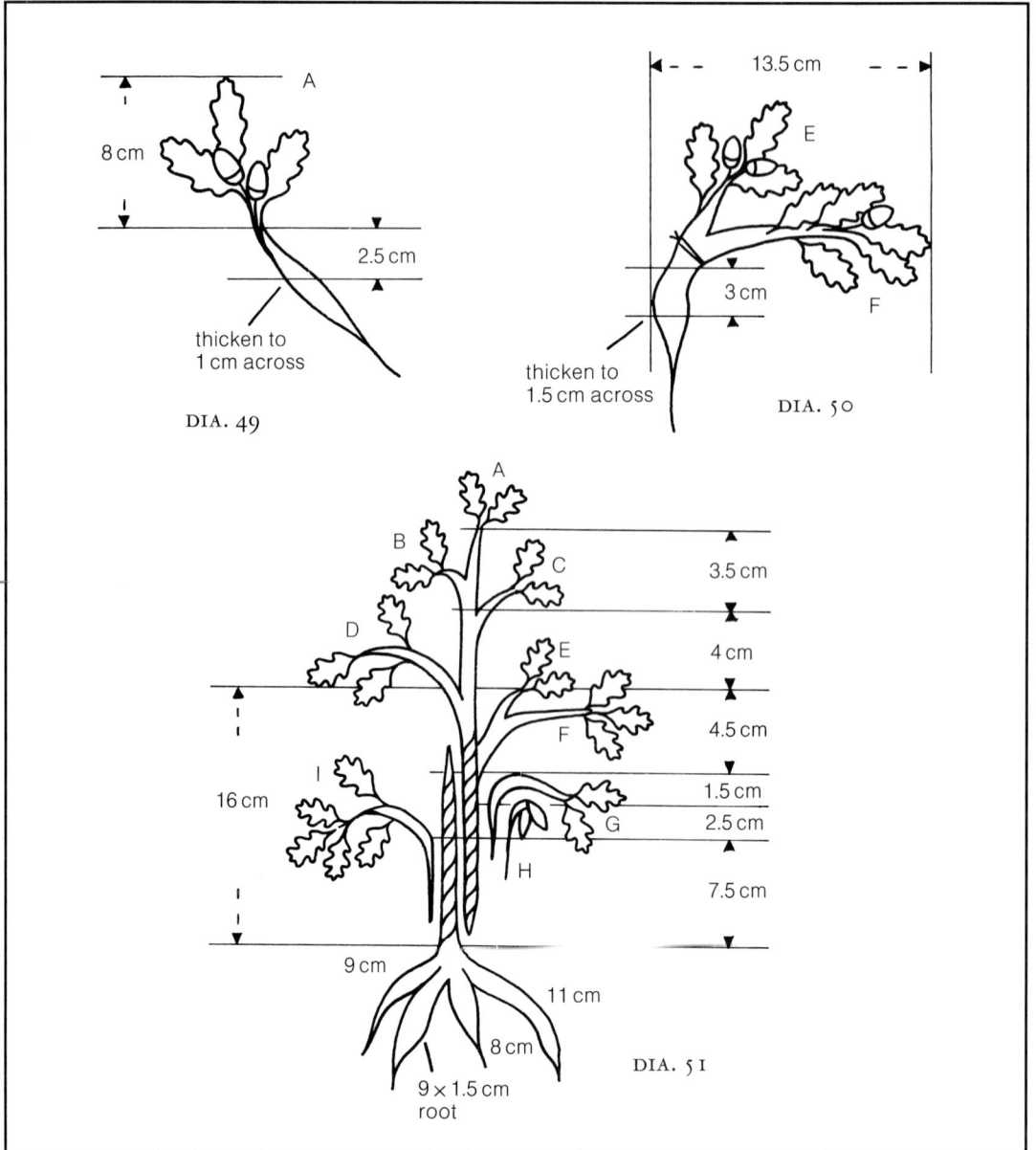

8 cm

A

2.5 cm

thicken to
1 cm across

DIA. 49

13.5 cm

E

3 cm

F

thicken to
1.5 cm across

DIA. 50

A

B

C

3.5 cm

D

4 cm

E

4.5 cm

F

1.5 cm

2.5 cm

G

16 cm

I

H

7.5 cm

9 cm

11 cm

8 cm

9 × 1.5 cm
root

DIA. 51

across, mark and taper.

Branch H

3 large leaves = 9.5 cm.* Thicken for 1 cm to 0.5 cm across, mark and taper.

Branch I

4 small + 3 medium + 2 large leaves = 15 cm.* Thicken for 2 cm to 1 cm across, mark and taper.

*From top of first leaf to base of last leaf.

Texture each branch with bonsai tape as in basic techniques and allow to dry.

Roots

Using basic techniques makes 4 roots in the following approximate sizes:

12 cm × 1.5 cm		8 cm	
12 cm × 1.5 cm	Wire together so	9 cm	to the
12 cm × 1 cm	that roots are	9 cm	tips
12 cm × 1 cm		11 cm	respectively

Wire and tape all 4 roots together firmly above the binding wire to form the trunk.

Clip the wires off about 12 cm from the roots.

Assembling the tree (Diagram 51)

Wire branches A and B together on the marks, and tape with stem tape.

Thicken again if necessary for 1 cm to 1.5 cm across, and cover with bonsai tape.

Using measurements on the diagram as an approximate guide, wire on branch C to the right. Thicken for 2.5 cm to 1.8 cm across. Add branch D, 4 cm below C to the left and slightly forwards.

At this point join the crown of the tree to the root section, overlapping the wires. Wire and tape firmly together. Note the position of the roots.

From the top, thicken for 2.5 cm to 2 cm across. Add E/F to the trunk, at the back and pointing to the right.

Check the position of the branches before making secure by looking down on the tree from above. All the branches should be visible; if necessary alter the position of E/F to comply with this.

Build up the trunk a little more with foil and stem tape. Cover with bonsai tape.

Add branch G to front right 2 cm below E/F, and branch H a fraction lower, slightly more forward.

Check the position of the branches again, and build up with foil and stem tape to 3 cm across. Cover with bonsai tape.

Add branch I to the left about 2.5 cm below G.

Again build up the trunk to 4 cm across at the base, finish in bonsai tape.

Finishing touches

Your little oak tree should now look straight and strong.

Plant the tree as in basic techniques. I chose a brown, dull-glazed bonsai dish from a local pottery for this tree, to complement the colour of the acorns.

Texture the trunk and roots as before with very pronounced ridging. Extra texturing where branches join the trunk may be moulded to give a more natural look.

Fill up any space in the dish with peat or compost mixture; a few pebbles will add interest.

Dab glue on the trunk, roots and soil area and sprinkle with lichen-coloured powder to simulate moss.

The oak should stand about 33 cm high from the table top.

11 Tulip Tree (*height 26 cm*)

CHINESE TULIP TREE (*MOKUREN*)
Semi-cascading style (*hai-kengai*)

Materials

75 cm Bensilky Ombre yellow No. 2 or No. 4
150 cm Bensilky green No. 5
35 cm Bensilky green No. 41
80 cm Satin Acetate No. 28 or 41
1 bundle pointed yellow stamens P58
Wires in gauges 30, 18 and 28 white, 24 green
Stem tape – nile green
Bonsai tape – grey (1 roll)
Wide double-sided tape.
Texturing materials

Flowers and buds

Petals and sepals

Make 6 petals 7.2 cm × 4.8 cm
9 petals 7.2 cm × 3.6 cm
3 petals 7.2 cm × 2.4cm

Make 3 sepals 6 cm × 3.6 cm
6 sepals 5 cm × 3.6 cm

Measure off the petals on the silky ombre with the light edge to the base. Line with double-sided tape, place a quarter-piece of 28 wire down the centre of the petal and back with green silky No. 5.

Cut to shape as Diagram 52 and shade as shown lightly with an orange felt pen on both sides.

Gather each petal in tightly at the base with 30 wire and tape with half-width nile stem tape. Stretch the tops of the petals to flare a little.

Make the sepals in the same way using green silky ribbon No. 5 backed with No. 41. Do not colour these.

Centres for flowers

On the end of a taped 18 wire, make a stigma approximately 2.5 cm long × 0.5 cm across in the middle, with tissue and stem tape.

Cut one end off about 50 stamens, and tape

these around the stigma so that they stand 1 cm above it. It is easier to do this in small groups and the stamens will be firmer and more evenly spaced (Diagram 53).

Make 3 centres in this way. A few less stamens

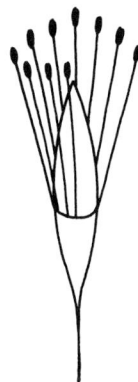

DIA. 53

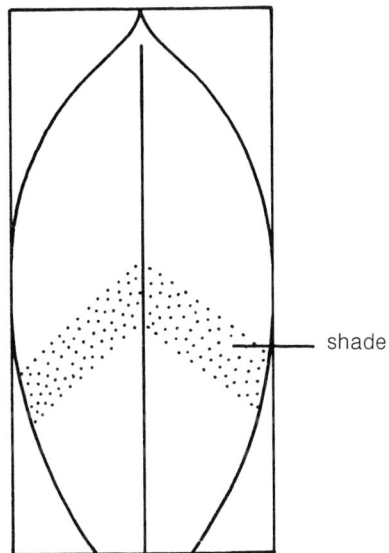

shade

DIA. 52

53

should be used for the smallest flower.

Assembling the flowers

For the large flower take a centre and tape 3 large petals evenly around it, green side out. Add 3 more petals in the spaces, and the 3 large sepals between those.

Pull the flower into a cupped shape, bending the petals outwards at the top.

For the medium flower tape 6 medium petals and 3 small sepals around the centre as above.

For the small flower tape the 3 small petals on first, followed by 3 medium petals, and the last 3 sepals.

Making the buds

On the end of a half-piece of taped 18 wire, make a bud approximately 3.6 cm long × 1 cm across with tissue and stem tape. Colour the tip with yellow felt pen.

Cut 3 light green sepals 3.6 cm × 1.8 cm and glue these around the bud to overlap. Cut 3 more in dark green and glue around the first 3. Neaten with stem tape (Diagram 54).

Make a second bud slightly larger.

Leaves

These unusual shaped leaves are slightly broader than they are long.

Make 6 leaves 4.5 cm × 3.6 cm
    4 leaves 7.2 cm × 6 cm
    4 leaves 8 cm × 7.2 cm

Measure off the green satin and line with wide double-sided tape. Place a half-piece of 24 wire down the centre and cut to shape (Diagram 55).

Tape the stems in nile green and mark veins with a pointed tool or heated iron.

Branches

First add an extra 18 wire to each flower stem to strengthen it – tape them together for the full length from just under the flower head.

Using half-width bonsai tape, add leaves with 3–4 cm of leaf stem. Space them down the branch to end up at the measurements given, thickening the branch proportionately between each addition.

Branch A
Large flower, add 1 small, 2 medium and 1 large leaf = 20 cm.* Thicken for a further 7 cm to 1.2 cm across, mark and taper.

Branch B
Medium flower, add 1 medium and 2 large leaves = 20 cm.* Thicken for a further 2.5 cm to 1.2 cm across, mark and taper.

Branch C
Small flower, add 2 small and 1 medium leaf = 17 cm.* Thicken for a further 6 cm to 1 cm across, mark and taper.

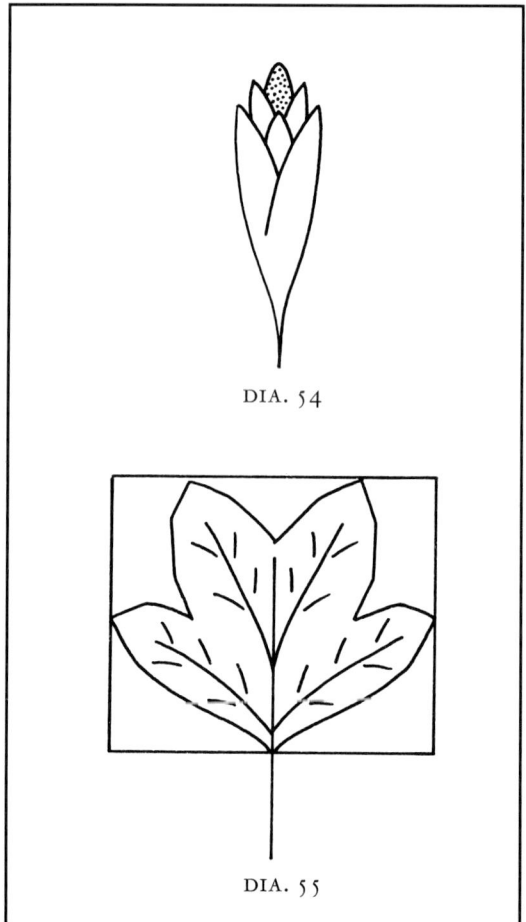

DIA. 54

DIA. 55

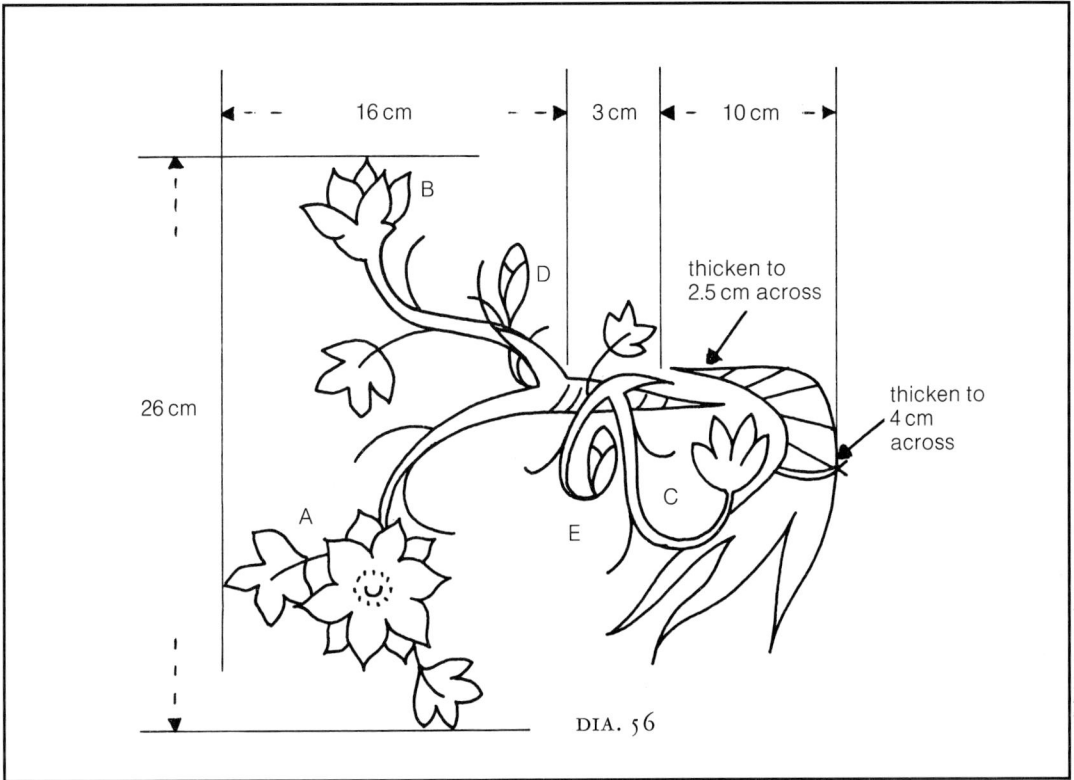

DIA. 56

Branch D
Large bud, add 1 small and 1 medium leaf = 11 cm.* Thicken a little for 1 cm and mark.

Branch E
Small bud, add 2 small leaves = 10 cm.* Thicken a little for 1 cm and mark.

The branches can be textured with bonsai tape before continuing if wished, keep the bark fairly smooth.

Roots

Make 3 roots as in basic methods to the following sizes:

$$
\left.\begin{array}{l}
17\,\text{cm} \times 1.6\,\text{cm} \\
17\,\text{cm} \times 1.4\,\text{cm} \\
17\,\text{cm} \times 1.2\,\text{cm}
\end{array}\right\}
\begin{array}{l}
\text{Wire together} \\
\text{so that roots} \\
\text{are}
\end{array}
\left\{\begin{array}{l}
16\,\text{cm} \\
12\,\text{cm} \\
14\,\text{cm}
\end{array}\right\}
\begin{array}{l}
\text{to the tips} \\
\text{respectively.}
\end{array}
$$

Tape together firmly above the binding wire to form the trunk.

Assembling the tree (Diagram 56)
Wire branches A and B together on the marks. Tape with bonsai tape and add the large bud (branch D) 1.5 cm below the join, at the back and to the left.

Wire and tape small bud (branch E) to branch C on the marks, add to the trunk at the back, 3 cm below D.

Bend the tree to shape (see diagram), bringing C/E over to front right. Since the flowers grow in a candelabra style, you must bear this in mind when arranging the tree for display.

Wire and tape the top of the tree to the root section. The thickest root should be to the left, and in the centre of the other two.

Trim the wires as necessary and bend the trunk over to the left. Thicken the trunk with foil to 4 cm across at the base, tapering to 2.5 cm across where the branches meet.

*From the top of the flower to the last leaf joint.

55

Finishing touches

Plant the tree as in basic techniques. My container this time is an authentic oblong bonsai dish 4.5 cm deep in a metallic grey-green green glaze.

Texture the tree with bonsai tape as before (the trunk has more pronounced ridges than the branches).

I used a peat mixture to fill up the dish, mounding it well up around the roots. Add a few pebbles for interest and glue plenty of lichen-coloured modelling powder onto the branches, trunk and root area.

The tulip tree stands 26 cm from the table top, with the lowest leaf slightly below the base of the dish.

JAPANESE MOUNTAIN MAPLE
(*YAMAMOMIJI*)
Semi-cascade style (*hai-kengai*)

Materials

2 m Roman Bensilky in autumnal shades
2 m Bensilky light brown No. 20
Wires in gauges 18 and 28 white
Stem tape – beige
Bonsai tape – brown (2 rolls)
Wide double-sided tape + glue or paste
Texturing materials

Leaves

Use various shades of ribbon for the best effect, I used roman silky Nos. 64, 81 and 83 all backed with plain No. 20. Make both dark and light leaves in each size.

Make leaves in two sizes:
31 from 3.6 cm squares
26 from 4.8 cm squares

Measure off the ribbon, and back with wide double-sided tape.

Place 28 wires as shown, using a 9 cm piece for the stem and bending a 3 cm piece to suit for each side. Press on the backing silk and cut to shape as in Diagram 57. Tape the stems with third-width stem tape, and lightly finger texture each leaf to take off the stiff look.

Branches

Sort the leaves into dark and light shades. Use dark ones mainly for branches A and B, and the light ones mainly for C and D. Make sure that leaves are used in blocks of a similar shade for each portion of the branch.

Allow 2 cm of stem on each leaf, use quarter-width bonsai tape, and join in a full piece of taped 18 wire with the third leaf.

Branch A – Diagram 58.
1. 4 small leaves + 2 large leaves = 11 cm.*
   Thicken a little for 2 cm.

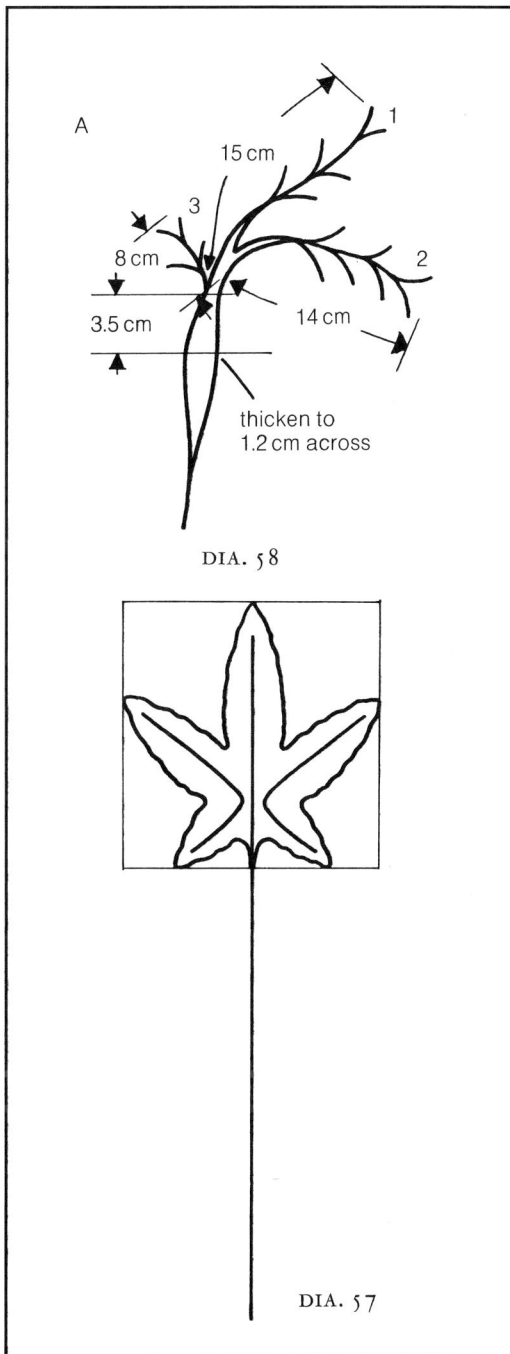

DIA. 58

DIA. 57

12 Mountain Maple (*height 40 cm*)

2. 4 small leaves + 3 large leaves = 11 cm.*
   Thicken a little for 1 cm. Join to 1 and
   thicken for 2 cm.

3. 2 small leaves + 2 large leaves = 8 cm.*
   (Does not need an 18 wire.) Join to 1 and 2.

Thicken the branch proportionately for a
further 3.5 cm to end up at 1.2 cm across,
mark and taper off below that measurement.

Branch B – Diagram 59.

1. 5 small leaves + 2 large leaves = 12.5 cm.*
   Thicken a little for 3 cm.

2. 3 small leaves + 1 large leaf = 9 cm.* (Does
   not need an 18 wire.) Thicken for 1 cm and
   join to 1. Thicken these two for further
   5 cm

*From the tip of the first leaf to the joint of the last leaf.

3. 4 small leaves + 2 large leaves = 13 cm.*
   Thicken for 4 cm and join to 1 and 2.

Thicken the branch for 2 cm to 0.8 cm across,
mark and taper as before.

Branch C – Diagram 60.

1. 3 small leaves + 3 large leaves = 10 cm.*
   Thicken for 5 cm.

2. 2 small leaves + 2 large leaves = 8 cm.*
   Thicken for 1.5 cm and join to 1.

3. 2 small + 3 large leaves = 11 cm.* Thicken
   for 4 cm and join to 1 and 2.

Thicken the branch for 7 cm to 1.5 cm across,
mark and taper as before.

Branch D – Diagram 61.

1. 1 small + 4 large leaves = 11 cm.* Thicken
   for 1.5 cm.

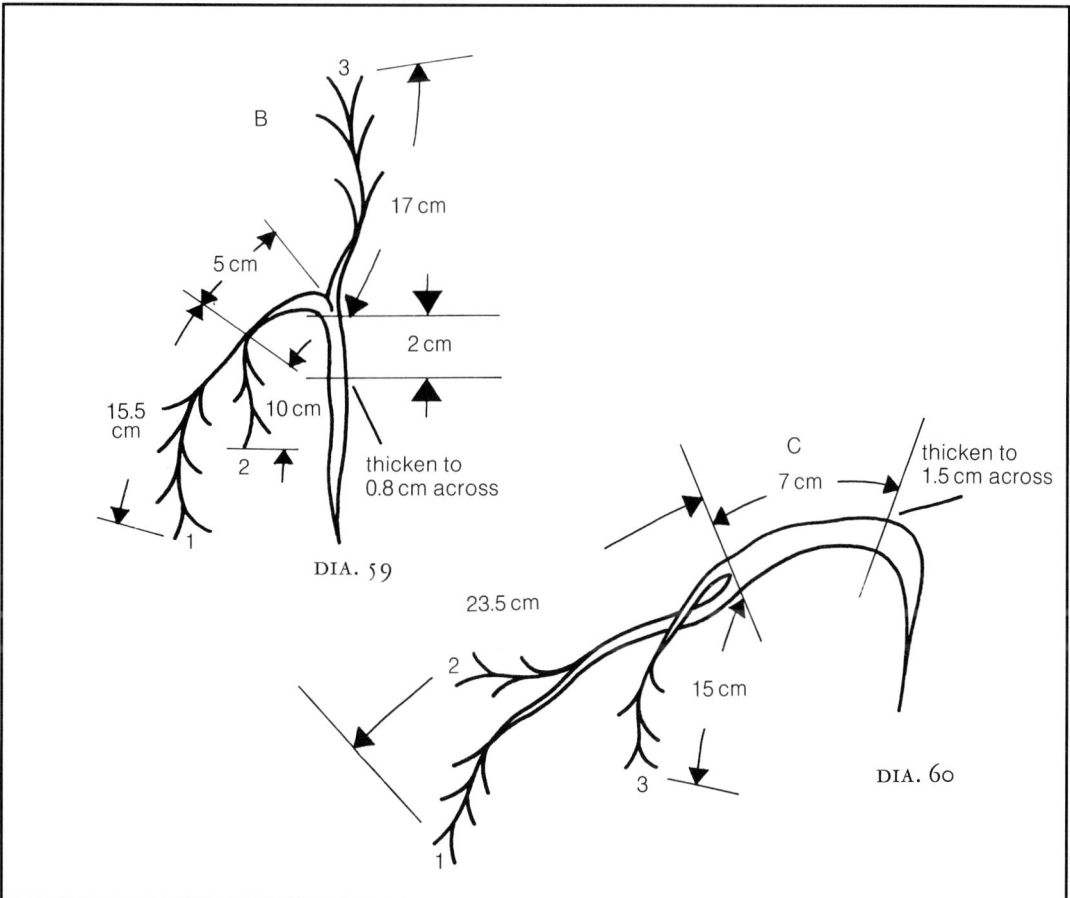

DIA. 59

DIA. 60

D

12.5 cm

9.5 cm

3.5 cm

thicken to
1 cm across

DIA. 61

A

B

D

C

4.5 cm

3 cm

26 cm

7 cm

8 cm

10 cm

DIA. 62

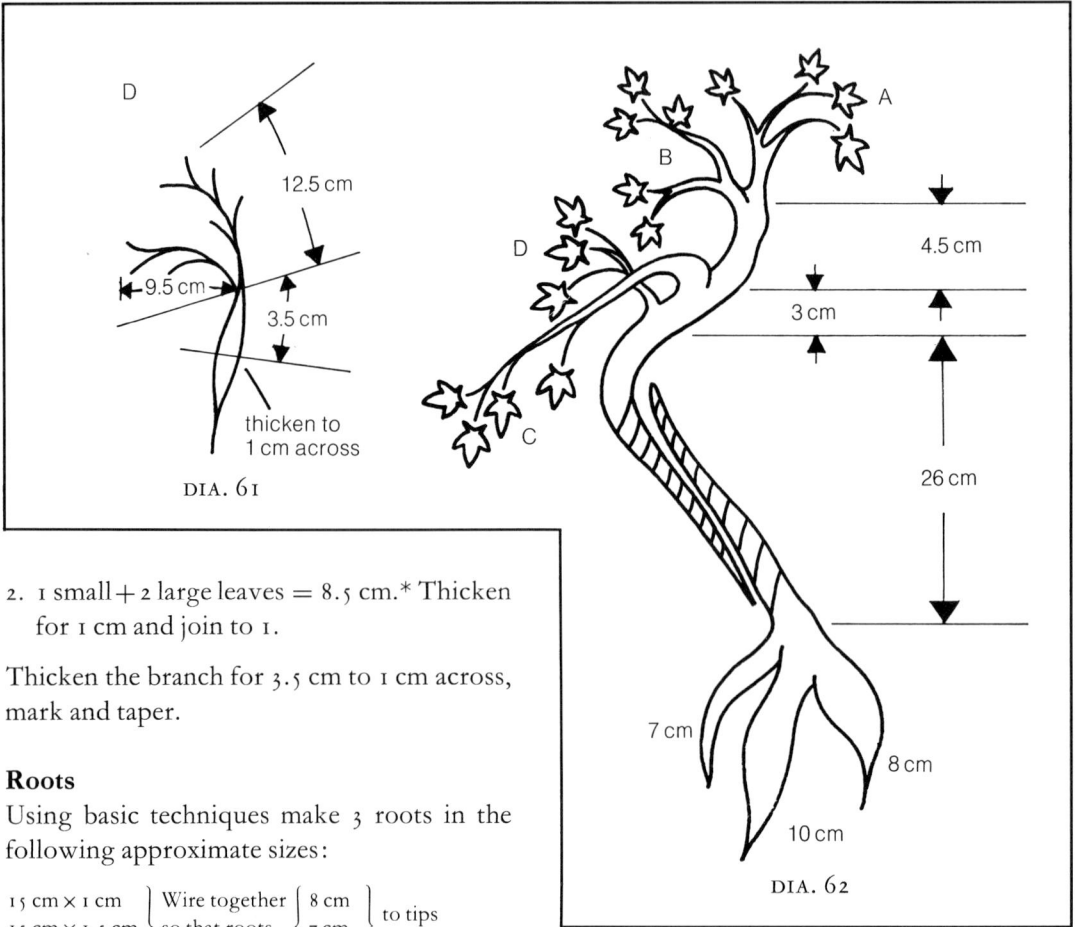

2. 1 small + 2 large leaves = 8.5 cm.* Thicken for 1 cm and join to 1.

Thicken the branch for 3.5 cm to 1 cm across, mark and taper.

Roots

Using basic techniques make 3 roots in the following approximate sizes:

15 cm × 1 cm	Wire together	8 cm	
15 cm × 1.5 cm	so that roots	7 cm	to tips
15 cm × 1.8 cm	are	10 cm	respectively.

Tape firmly above the wire.

Assembling the tree (Diagram 62)

Wire branches A and B together, with A in front of B. Wrap with half-width bonsai tape.

4.5 cm lower add branch C to left front, wire and tape as before.

3 cm below that add branch D to left and slightly back.

Try to shape the tree as you go to give a nice curve. Looking down from the top, check the position of the branches so that they can all be seen.

Join the top of tree to the roots, position the longest and thickest root to the left and between the other two. When extended the trunk will measure 26 cm from branch D to the roots.

Finishing touches

A deeper container is usually required for this style of bonsai. I have used a cork-textured stoneware dish 6.5 cm deep. Placing the dish on a stand helps to give the right impression.

Fill the dish half-full with plaster of paris, to give weight. The roots can be pressed into this while it is still soft, or it can be left to dry and the tree then planted in the normal way on top of the plaster. Bend and twist the trunk so that the lower branches of the maple cascade down to the left, with the tip of the lowest branch almost touching the table.

Build up the trunk with foil and stem tape to 3.5 cm across for the lower 5 cm; taper to just under 2 cm across higher up – not necessarily evenly. The more gnarled the trunk can be made to look the better. Wrap with full-width bonsai tape, then, using short lengths of bonsai tape and paste, texture as described before. While still wet, sprinkle brown modelling powder over most of the tree and leave to dry thoroughly.

Paint the clay or plaster in the dish brown.

Make up some of the peat mixture to fill up the dish and mound it up around but not over the roots. Any large cracks can be filled in with more mixture when the first application has dried out.

Green lichen-coloured powder can now be used around the base of the tree, over the roots and to highlight the trunk. Cork granules or a few small pebbles can be added to the soil surface for interest.

The maple should measure about 40 cm high from the table top.

13 White Pine (*height 38 cm*)

WHITE PINE (*GOYA-MATSU*)
Rock-grown, windswept style (*ishitsuki, fukinagashi*)

Materials
Wires in gauges 18, 30 and 28 dark green; 26 lime green
Stem tape – beige
Bonsai tape – grey (1 roll)
Glue or paste
Texturing materials
Dried natural lichen
Suitable piece of rock or stone

Pine Needle units
Cut some dark and light green wires into 6 cm lengths. Take 3 pieces of the same colour, bind them together in the middle with a short length of 30 wire (Diagram 63).

Bend the ends together and tape the base with half-width stem tape (Diagram 64).

Make 60 units in light green, and 180 units in dark green.

Make a small bud end on quarter-piece of 26 wire with beige tape, and tape down the wire.

Tape 2 units of light green needles around the bud, and 4 units of dark green needles around that a fraction lower (Diagram 65).

Use quarter-width bonsai tape over the base of the lower needles and tape down to the end of the wire.

Make 40 of these groups – a few all dark green.

Branches
First make storm-damaged (jinned) branches on half-pieces of 18 wire thickened with tissue and stem tape. Finish and texture in bonsai tape (Diagrams 66 and 67).

Using quarter-width bonsai tape make up groups of pine needles into twigs without any extra reinforcing wire. The number in the circle on the diagrams denotes the number of pine needle groups on a twig.

Wire and tape the twigs together as in Diagrams 68, 69 and 70, adding a taped 18 wire where necessary. Incorporate jinned branch X with top branch A.

Thicken, texture and mark each branch before continuing.

Roots
Make the roots as in basic techniques. For this style of tree the length and shape of the roots depend on the rock being used.

I made 6 long roots on full-length 18 wires, the thickest being 1 cm across near the base of the tree. Some roots I divided near the base of the rock. To do this use 2 wires and start the roots as usual, join the 2 wires together 10 cm from the ends and then treat as one root.

Arrange the roots over the rock and mark their positions with chalk. Wire the roots

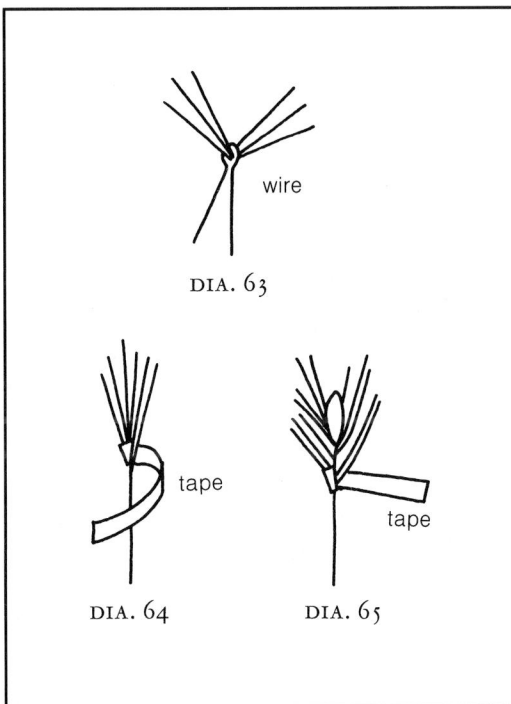

wire

DIA. 63

tape

DIA. 64

tape

DIA. 65

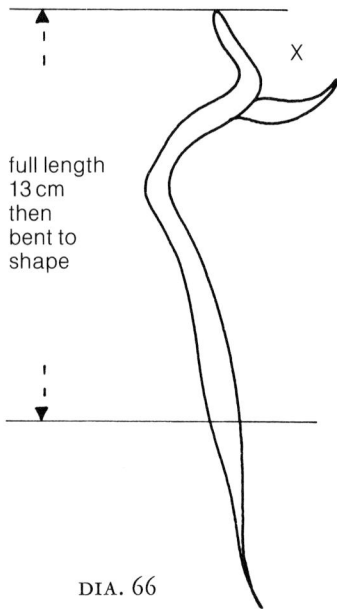

full length
13 cm
then
bent to
shape

X

DIA. 66

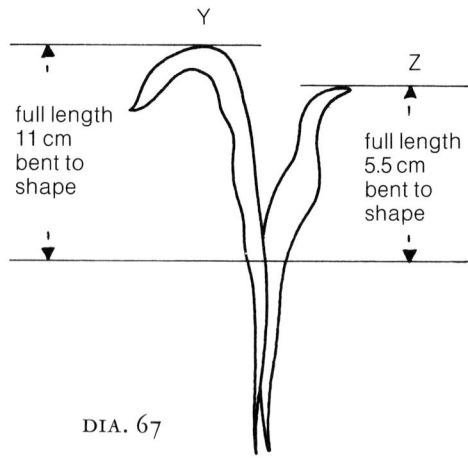

Y

full length
11 cm
bent to
shape

Z

full length
5.5 cm
bent to
shape

DIA. 67

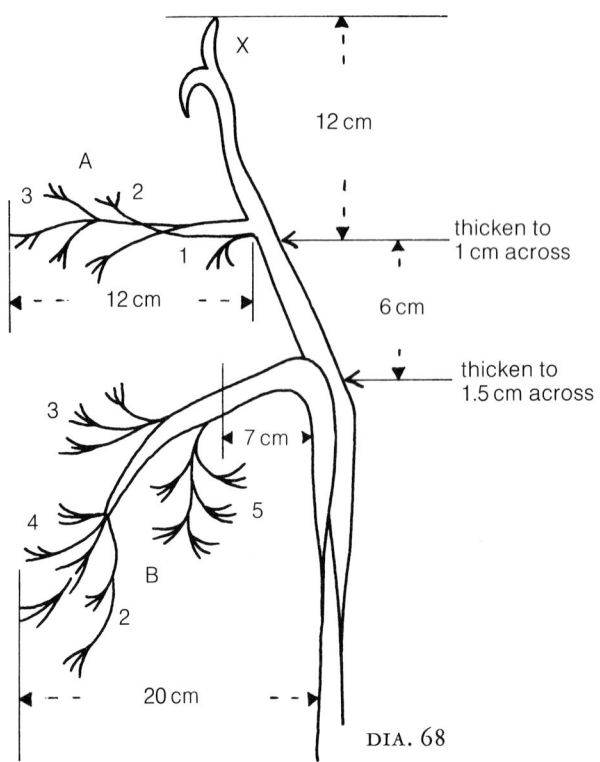

X

12 cm

thicken to
1 cm across

A

3   2

1

12 cm

6 cm

thicken to
1.5 cm across

3

7 cm

4   5

B

2

20 cm

DIA. 68

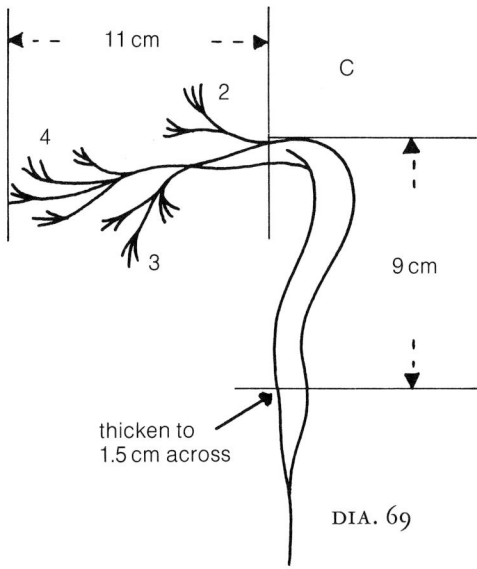

DIA. 69

11 cm

C

2

4

3

9 cm

thicken to
1.5 cm across

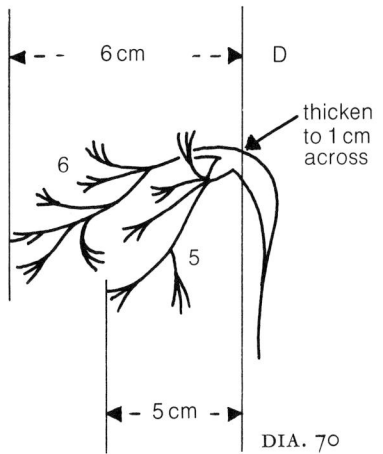

DIA. 70

6 cm

D

thicken
to 1 cm
across

6

5

5 cm

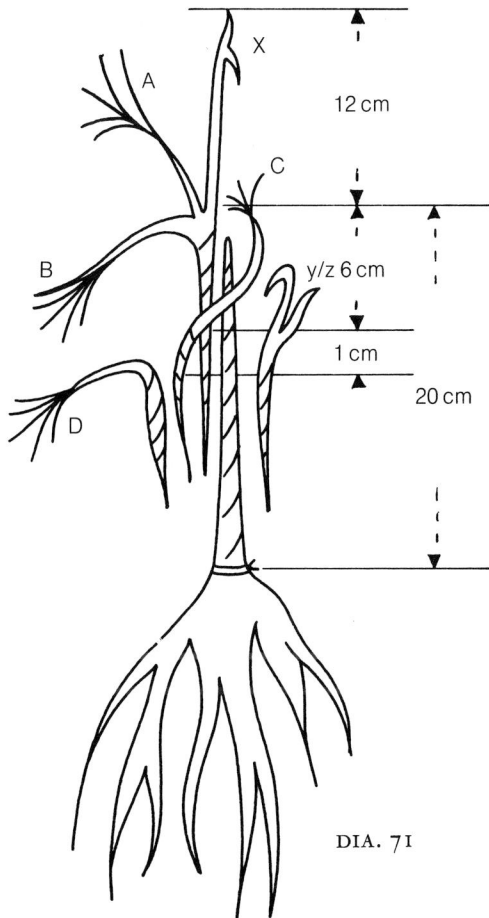

DIA. 71

X

A

C

B

D

y/z 6 cm

12 cm

1 cm

20 cm

firmly together where they meet on the top of the rock; wire and tape the excess wires together to form the trunk.

Assembling the tree (Diagram 71)

Following the measurements in Diagram 68 wire branch B to A/X and thicken to 1.5 cm across.

Wire and tape this section of the tree to the root section, overlapping the wires to form the trunk. This should measure 20 cm from branch B to the top of the roots.

Then, following Diagram 71, 6 cm below B place branch C to the front of the trunk, wire on tightly and then bend C up and around the back of the trunk to the left.

1 cm below C add branch D to front left, and jinned branches Y/Z to the right side a little lower. 6 cm below these bend the trunk over to the left.

Build up the trunk with foil, varying the thickness from 3 cm to 4 cm across. Bind with bonsai tape and texture as before.

Finishing touches

Place the pine on top of the rock, spreading the roots over the chalk marks for guidance and tuck the ends under the rock.

Make sure the tree is leaning to the left as if blown by the wind; arrange the branches with the same idea in mind.

Stand the rock in a shallow dish. I used a deep dinner plate, and placed the rock to one side.

Make up some peat or compost mixture and heap it up around the base of the rock. Use fine gravel on the edge to represent scree.

Dab glue and grey modelling powder on the trunk, branches and exposed roots. Dried lichen stuck on the trunk, roots and rock is also very effective and gives an authentic touch.

The tree is about 38 cm high from the table top, but this may vary a little depending on the size of the rock.

FLOWERING CHERRY (*FUJI-SAKURA*)
In the cascading style (*kengai*)

Materials

5 m Bensilky in assorted pinks
1.5 m Roman Bensilky green No. 66
1.5 m Bensilky green No. 29
25 cm Bensilky light brown No. 20
Wires in gauges 18, 30 and 24 green; 28 covered
Stem tape – nile green and olive green
Bonsai tape – brown (2 rolls)
5 mm double-sided tape + glue or paste
Cotton wool
Cone of dry oasis, and prong
Texturing materials

Flowers and buds

Cut the pink silky into 5 cm squares and shape petals as in Diagram 72.

Make the florettes in 3 sizes, using either half a petal, 1 petal or 2 petals as follows:

Gather the petal(s) in the centre, twist wire with 30 wire leaving a stem of 5 cm, tape in half-width nile green (Diagram 73).

Make the buds by rolling a small piece of cotton wool into a ball. Cover with a small square of silky, gather together and twist wire as florettes.

Cut a green calyx as pattern from 2.4 cm squares (Diagram 74). Wrap around the bud, wire and tape in place.

You will need about 75 florettes in assorted sizes and 20–25 buds.

Leaves

Make leaves in the following sizes:
45 leaves 5 cm × 1.8 cm
15 leaves 6 cm × 2 cm
10 leaves 7.2 cm × 2.4 cm

Measure off the ribbon using the roman silky with the light edge to the top.

Stick narrow double-sided tape down the centre of each section, place third-piece of 24 wire onto the tape and back with the plain green silky. Cut to shape as in Diagram 75.

Texture each leaf with the handkerchief method and tape the stems in olive green.

Assembling flower units

Using quarter-width bonsai tape, make about 30 units by taping together 2 or 3 flowers

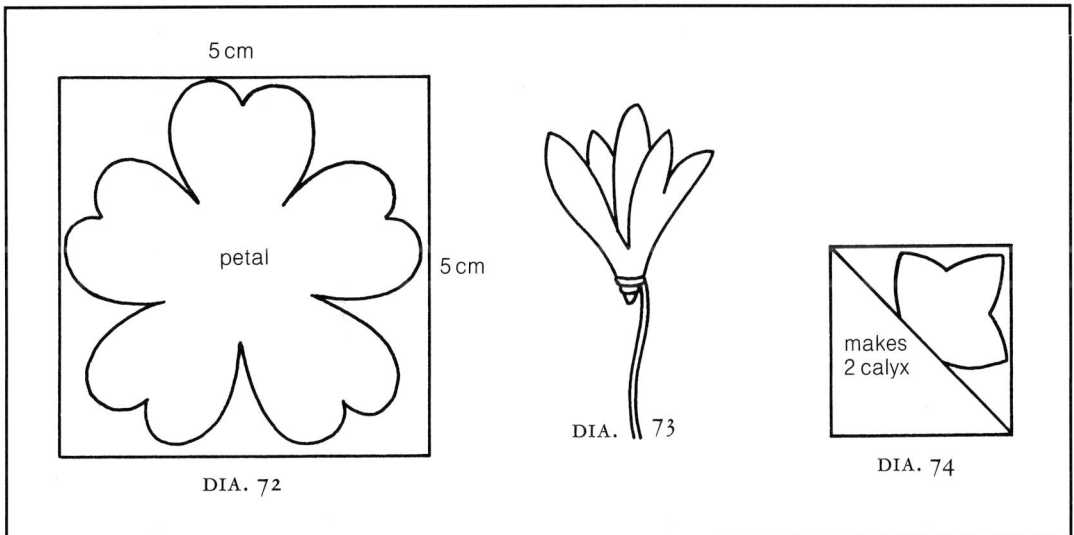

5 cm

petal

5 cm

DIA. 72

DIA. 73

makes
2 calyx

DIA. 74

14 Flowering Cherry (*overall height 38 cm*)

and/or buds with 1 or 2 leaves. Vary the length of the stems.

Cut calyx in brown from 3.6 cm squares, wire and tape onto each unit (Diagram 76).

20 leaves should be left for use when making the branches.

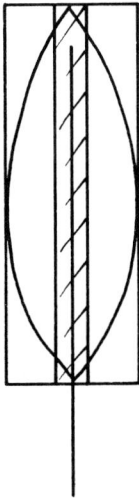

DIA. 75

DIA. 76

Branches

Join the flower units together onto 18 wire, using quarter-width bonsai tape and following the measurements given for each branch.

Lower branch A – Diagram 77.
Section 1 – Tape 5 units on 18 wire = 15 cm.* Thicken proportionately for further 6.5 cm, mark and taper off.

Section 2 – Tape 18 wire with a bud end, add 5 units = 16 cm.* Thicken for 2 cm, mark and taper off.
Section 3 – Tape 4 units on 18 wire = 14 cm.* Thicken for proportionately for 5.5 cm, mark and taper off.

Join these 3 sections together on the marks with wire and tape. Thicken for 5 cm to 1.5 cm across, mark and taper off.

Centre branch B – Diagram 78.
Section 1 – Tape 18 wire with bud end, add 3 units = 14 cm.* Thicken proportionately for 7 cm, mark and taper.

Section 2 – Tape 18 wire with bud end, add 4 units = 15 cm.* Thicken proportionately for 4.5 cm, mark and taper.

Section 3 – Thicken 1 unit a little for 2 cm, mark.

Join these 3 sections together on the marks with wire and tape adding 4 extra leaves.

Thicken for 4 cm to 1.5 cm across.

Top branch C – Diagram 79.
Section 1 – Tape 18 wire with bud end, add 4 units with an extra green bud = 16 cm.*

Section 2 – Tape 2 units on 18 wire = 9 cm.*

Wire these 2 together 1.5 cm below the last joint on each section. Thicken for a further 4 cm, mark and taper.

Section 3 – Tape 18 wire with bud end, add 2 units + 3 extra leaves = 12 cm.* Thicken for 4 cm, mark and taper.

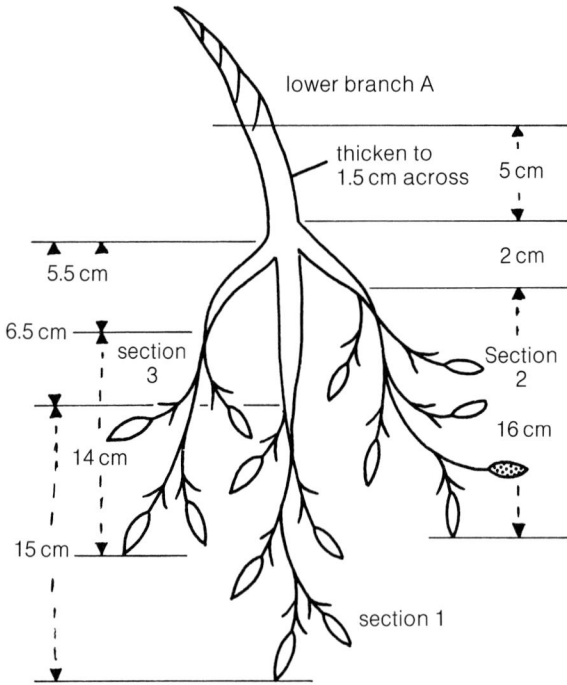

lower branch A

thicken to
1.5 cm across

5 cm

2 cm

5.5 cm

6.5 cm

section
3

Section
2

16 cm

14 cm

15 cm

section 1

DIA. 77

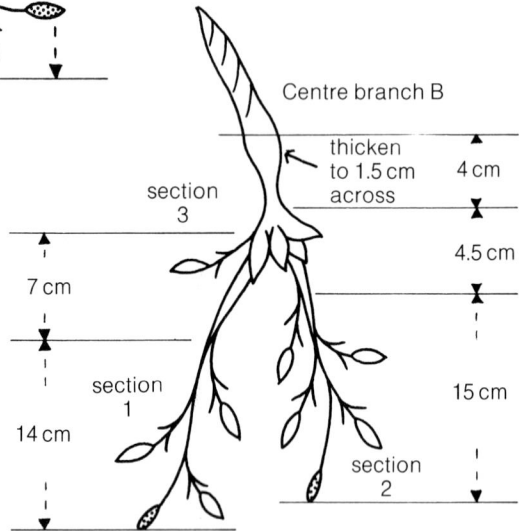

Centre branch B

thicken
to 1.5 cm
across

4 cm

4.5 cm

section
3

7 cm

15 cm

section
1

14 cm

section
2

DIA. 78

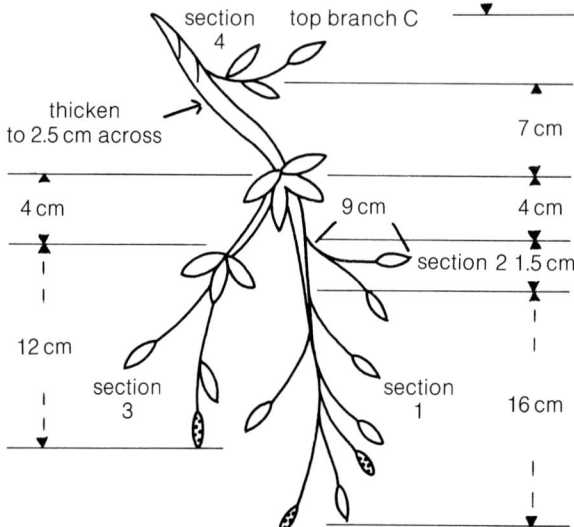

section
4

top branch C

thicken
to 2.5 cm across

7 cm

4 cm

4 cm

9 cm

section 2 1.5 cm

12 cm

section
3

section
1

16 cm

DIA. 79

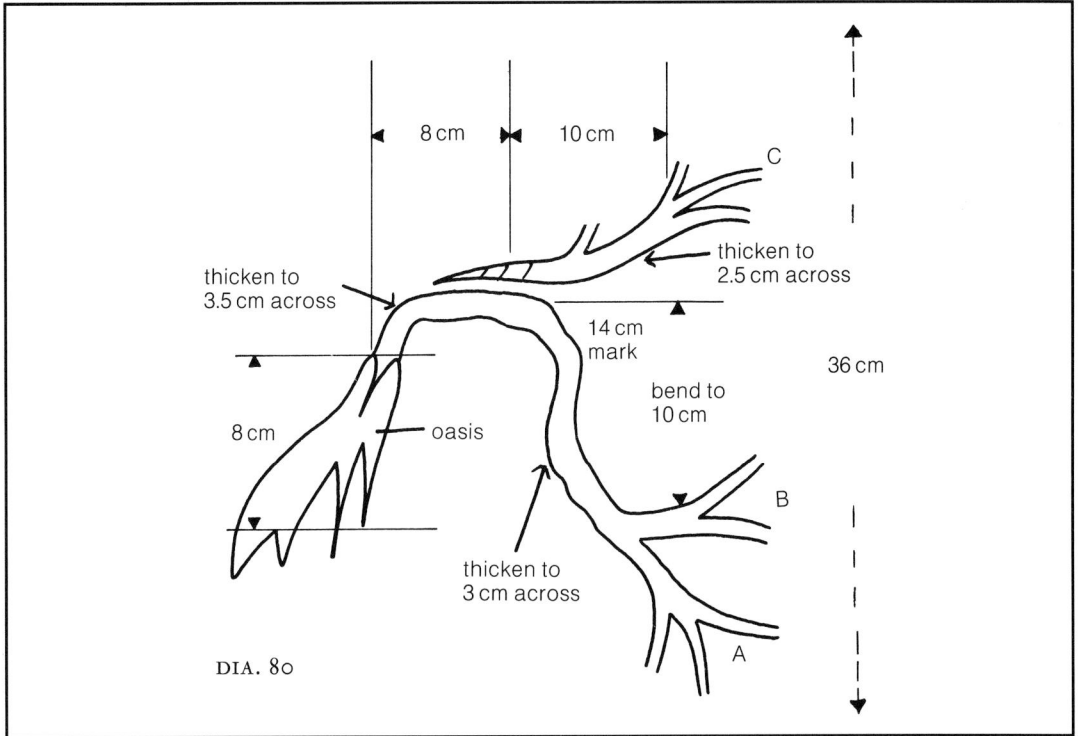

8 cm

10 cm

thicken to
2.5 cm across

C

thicken to
3.5 cm across

14 cm
mark

36 cm

bend to
10 cm

8 cm

oasis

thicken to
3 cm across

B

A

DIA. 80

Join the first 2 sections to section 3 on the marks with 4 extra leaves.

Section 4 – Tape 9 leaves on 18 wire = 12 cm.* Leave this section separate for the moment.

It is important to check each branch and if necessary thicken proportionately. It is also easier to texture the branches before continuing.

Roots

The roots for this tree are made in a different method to previous bonsai.

A deeper container is needed for this style, so first carve the oasis into a rough cone shape about $1\frac{1}{2}$ times the height of the pot.

Secure the oasis with a prong in the bottom of the pot, and fill any space with plaster to give weight.

Carve the oasis into a shape to simulate the

*From tip of first leaf to lowest joint.

top of the roots as they become the trunk.

Assembling the tree (Diagram 80)

Use bonsai tape in suitable widths for binding.

Wire branches A and B together on the marks and thicken with foil for 14 cm to 3 cm across; mark at this point.

Bend and shape this lower section, adding more foil if necessary to give a gnarled effect. Tape first with stem tape and finish in bonsai.

Thicken top branch C with foil for 10 cm to 2.5 cm across, join in the leaf section 4, 7 cm down.

Wire C to A and B at 10 cm and 14 cm marks and bind firmly in a criss-cross fashion with bonsai tape.

Thicken with foil for 8 cm to 3.5 cm across. Bend the tree to shape before pushing the wires from the branches below the 8 cm point into the top of the oasis cone.

71

Finishing touches

Pad the join of the crown and root section with foil, and bind with full-width bonsai tape down to the base, pinning it with small hairpins made from wire into the hollows.

Texture with bonsai tape as before. Cracks can be made in the bark to expose the bare trunk by lifting the edges of the texturing strips away from the trunk and inserting a small strip of grey or beige bonsai tape underneath.

The trunk and root area can be given extra texturing with modelling powder, and the surface around the roots covered with dried moss.

The height of the cherry is about 28 cm from the table top, but the lowest branches should cascade well down below the table edge by about 8 cm.

JAPANESE APRICOT (*UME*)
This Bonsai is a combination of three styles

The informal upright (myogi), which also has semi-cascading tendencies (hai-kengai). The small tree at the base brings it into the twin trunk or mother and daughter category (sokan).

Materials
35 cm Bensilky Ivory No. 61
25 cm Bensilky Apricot No. 63 or 64
25 cm Bensilky Light Brown No. 20
Cream-pointed stamens P4
Cream/Beige round stamens PT3
Wires in gauges 18 and 24 covered and 28 covered
Stem tape – beige
Bonsai tape – brown (2 rolls)
Texturing materials

Flower and buds
Cut the silky for the petals as pattern in Diagram 81 in the following sizes:

Ivory   –   6 from 3.6 cm squares
Ivory   – 19 from 2.4 cm squares
Apricot – 16 from 2.4 cm squares
Light brown – 25 from 1.8 cm squares, for the calyx

Cup the centre of the petals and calyx (a flower iron is useful here). Each separate petal section on the 3.6 cm size also needs cupping.

DIA. 81

Make 2 sizes of flowers as follows:

6 large flowers – Cut 3 P4 stamens in half and tape together with beige tape directly under the heads.

Make a hole in the centre of an apricot petal, dab with a little glue and pass the stamen stems through.

Take a 3.6 cm ivory petal, make a hole, dab with glue and slide up behind the first petal.

Repeat with a brown calyx.

10 small flowers – Make as above, using 3 stamens then a 2.4 cm apricot petal, followed by a 2.4 cm ivory petal then a calyx.

9 buds – Make by using a 2.4 cm ivory petal gathered up around the stamens; repeat with a calyx.

Being a little more generous with the glue will help to stick the petals in a semi-closed shape.

Branches
First cut the bonsai tape in half, then each half into three.

Following the branch chart for composition and measurements, take a whole piece of 24 wire and tape on half-stamens with flowers and buds as shown in Diagram 82.

Tape the wires together in pairs as indicated, thickening each with a little tape.

When all the pairs for a branch have been completed, wire together adding a half-piece of 18 wire at this point. Thicken as shown in example (see Diagram 83) to the measurements given on the branch chart. Finish in bonsai tape.

Make two pruned branch stumps on half-pieces of 18 wire. Make one 3 cm long and one 3.5 cm long, each thickened to 1 cm across. Flatten the tops and finish in bonsai tape.

73

15 Japanese Apricot (*height 50 cm*)

Branch chart

L = Large flower; S = Small flower;
B = Bud; H = Half-stamens

A 1 3H+L+2H = 15 cm
     6H   = 13 cm

  2 5H   = 12 cm
     2H+B+3H = 10 cm

  3 3H+S+2H = 13 cm
     6H   = 10 cm

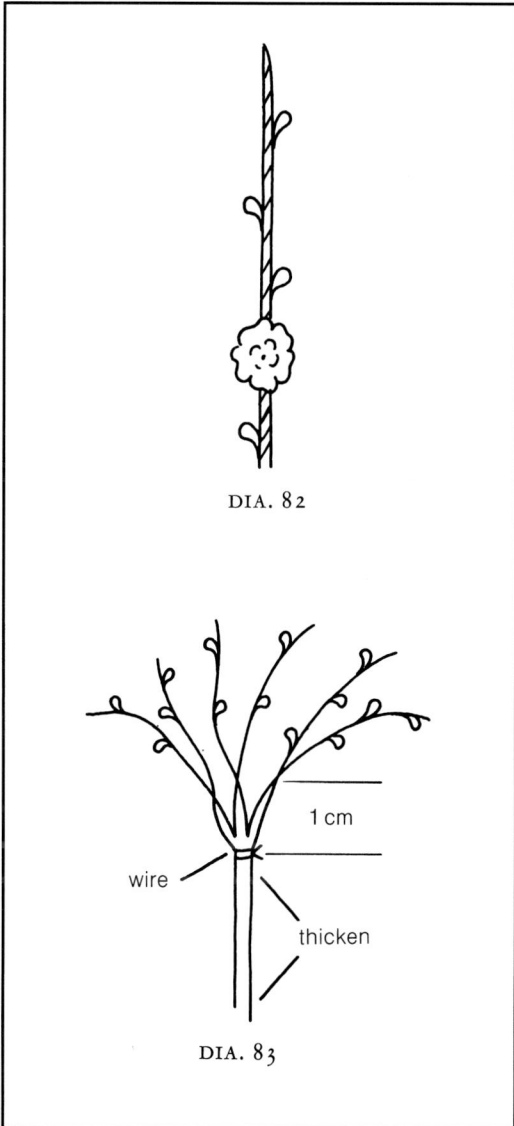

DIA. 82

1 cm

wire

thicken

DIA. 83

4 5H   = 10 cm
   5H   = 9 cm

5 5H   = 11 cm
   5H   = 10 cm

B 1 3H+L+3H+S+4H = 25 cm
     11H   = 20 cm

  2 4H+B+3H+S+4H = 28 cm
     10H   = 23 cm

  3 5H+B+11H = 24 cm
     11H   = 20 cm

C 1 5H+S+2H+L+3H = 27 cm
     11H   = 23 cm

  2 3H   = 13 cm
     3H+S+2H = 9 cm

  3 6H   = 15 cm
     3H+S+2H = 9 cm

D 1 5H+L+6H = 26 cm
     12H   = 27 cm

  2 8H+S+4H = 25 cm
     8H   = 27 cm

  3 18H   = 31 cm
     12H   = 23 cm

E 1 3H+B+2H = 14 cm
     6H   = 12 cm

  2 6H+B+2H+S+2H = 25 cm
     11H   = 22 cm

  3 4H+B+7H = 22 cm
     17H   = 29 cm

Thicken all these branches to 0.7 cm across.

F 1 12H+L+3H = 29 cm
     18H   = 28 cm

  2 5H+B+3H+S+4H = 22 cm
     11H   = 16 cm

  3 4H+S+3H+L+3H = 27 cm
     12H   = 23 cm

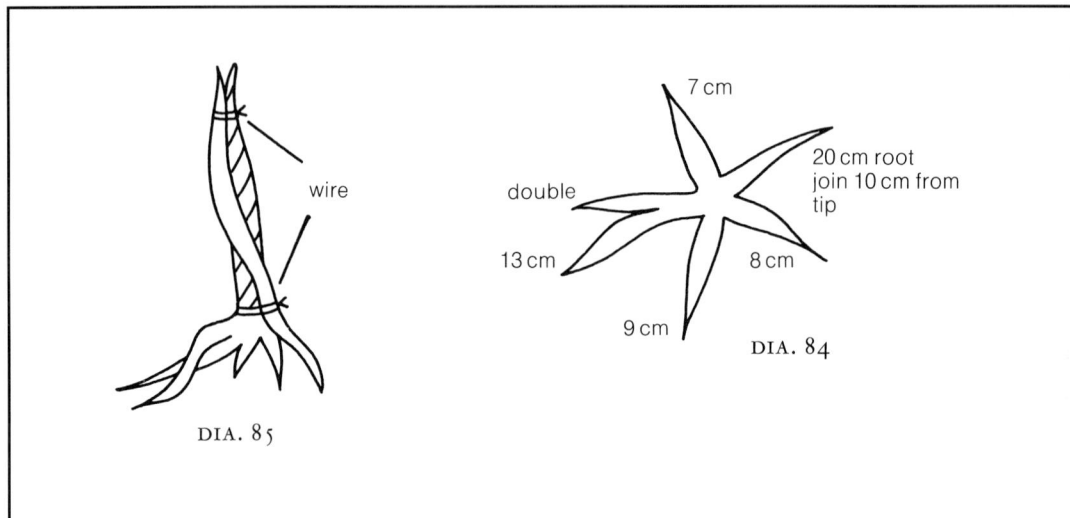

wire

double

7 cm

20 cm root
join 10 cm from
tip

13 cm

8 cm

9 cm

DIA. 84

DIA. 85

Thicken to 1 cm across.

G 1 4H+S+2H = 14 cm
    5H   = 12 cm

  2 3H+B+2H = 14 cm
     5H   = 12 cm

  3 6H   = 14 cm
    6H   = 17 cm

Thicken to 0.8 cm across

Roots

Using basic techniques make 1 double root as follows:

Make 2 roots 15 cm × 0.8 cm, wire them together 10 cm from the tips. Thicken for 3 cm to 1.2 cm across, finish in bonsai tape and twist one root over the other.

Make 4 roots:

10 cm × 1.5 cm		9 cm	to tips
10 cm × 1 cm	Wire together	8 cm	respectively.
10 cm × 0.8 cm	so that roots	7 cm	Position as
20 cm × 1.5 cm	are	10 cm	in Diagram
Double root		13 cm	84.

Bind the double and the 3 shorter roots together above the join with stem tape.

Bring the 20 cm root in front of and across to the other side to form the basis of a twisted trunk. Wire and bind together about 14 cm above the roots (Diagram 85).

Assembling the parent tree (Diagram 86)
Join the branches together with wire and stem tape as in the diagram as far as branch E. Use bonsai tape for the final coverage.

Check the position of the branches from above. Some texturing could be done at this stage.

Make up branch F/G but do not join in yet

Wire the crown of the tree to the root section. The trunk should measure 35 cm from branch E to the top of the roots.

Tape firmly and bend the trunk to shape. Wire in branch F/G to the left on the bend and thicken to 2 cm across at that point (Diagram 87).

Using foil, build up the trunk section to 4 cm across, moulding it into the twisted section and forming a gnarled shape.

Bind with bonsai tape and texture with short lengths of tape, giving the trunk a well-ridged appearance. Take care not to fill in the hollows.

76

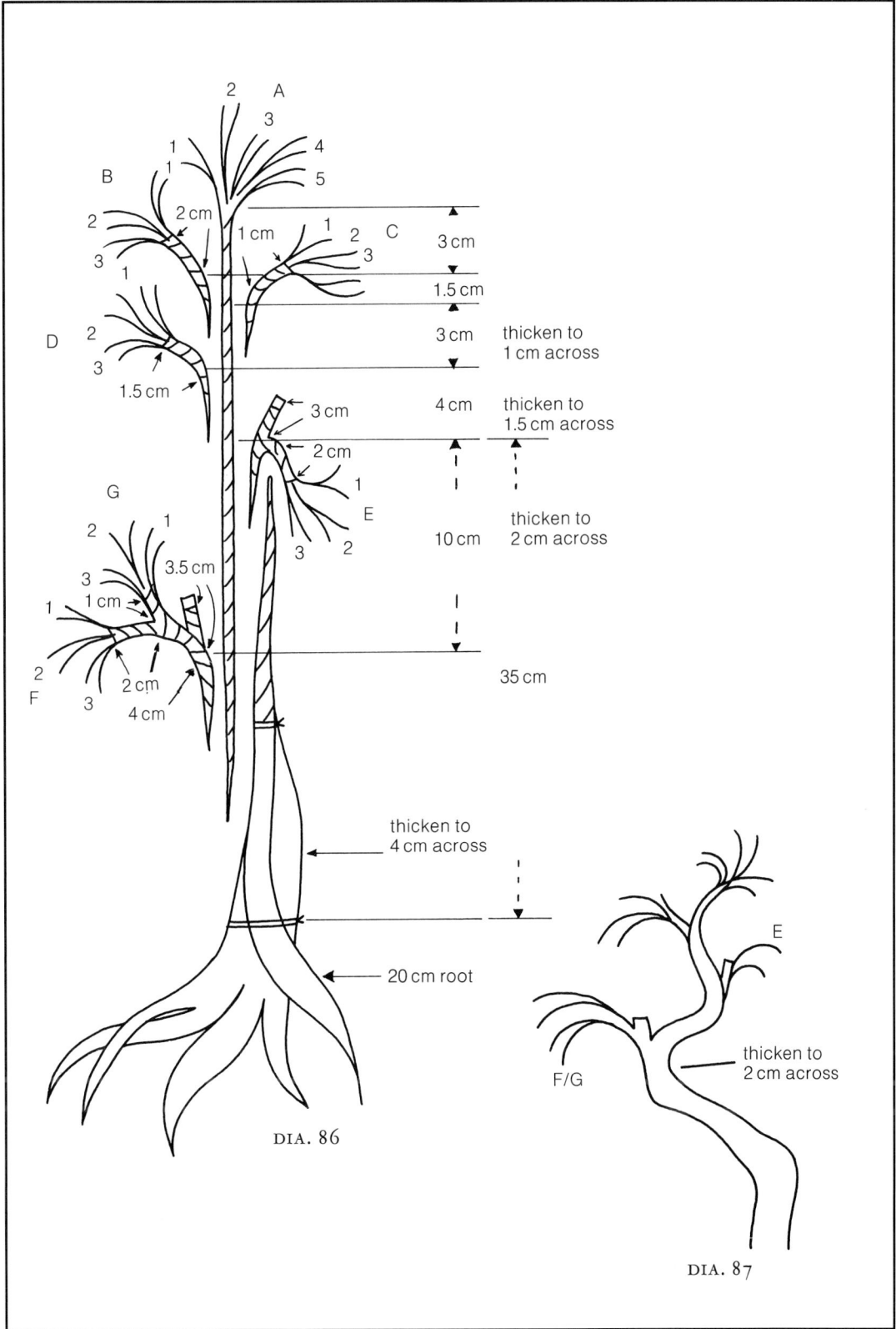

DIA. 86

DIA. 87

2
A
3
1
4
1
5
B
2 2 cm
3 1 cm 1 2 C
1 3
3 cm
1.5 cm
D 2 3 cm thicken to
3 1 cm across
1.5 cm
3 cm 4 cm thicken to
2 cm 1.5 cm across
1
E
thicken to
G 2 cm across
2 1 10 cm
3 3.5 cm
1 1 cm 3 2
2 35 cm
F 3 2 cm
4 cm
thicken to
4 cm across
20 cm root
E
F/G thicken to
2 cm across

DIA. 88

DIA. 89

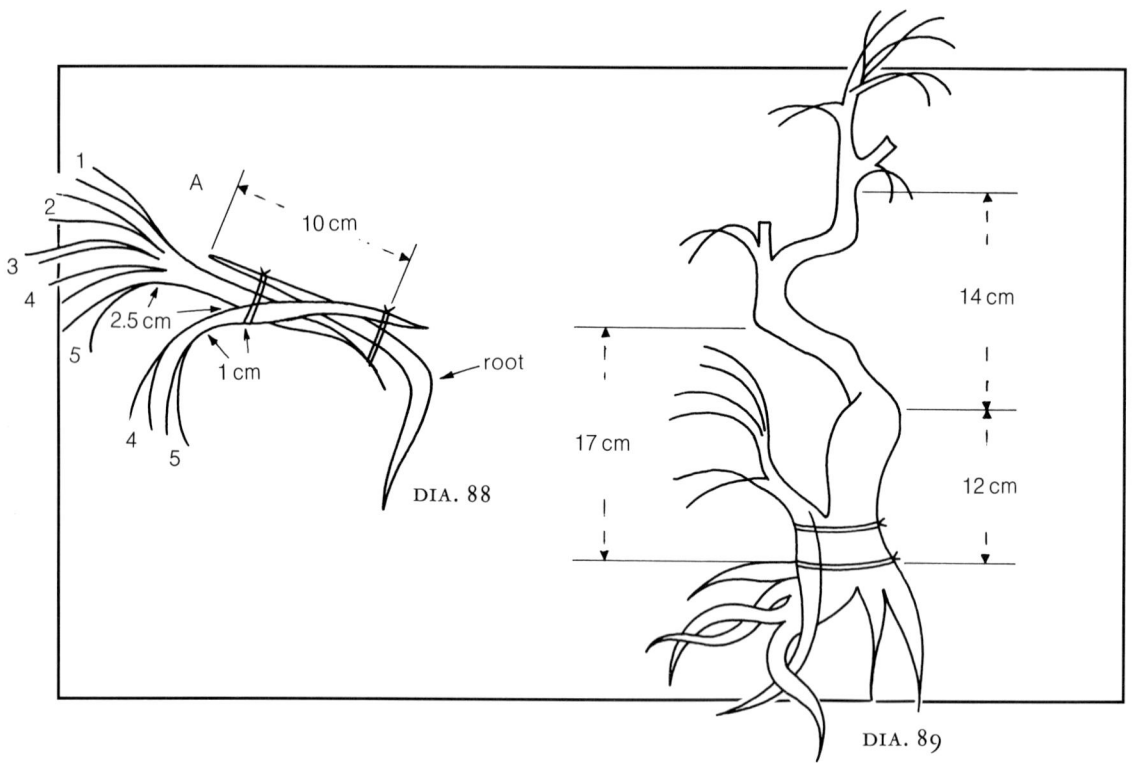

Daughter tree (Diagram 88)

Using half-pieces of 24 wire make branch A of the parent tree without flowers and thicken to 1.2 cm across.

Repeat sections 4 and 5 of branch A, thicken to 0.8 cm across.

Make a root 16 cm × 1 cm.

Wire branch A section to the root and tape firmly. Add smaller branch section on the left 2.5 cm down from A.

Wire at the top and twist the lower end round the trunk of the daughter tree as in the diagram. Wire at the base, tape and texture as before, moulding the tape into the hollows.

Finishing touches

Place the daughter tree comfortably in at the base of the parent tree.

Wire together at the base and again 2 cm higher up. Twist the root with the 9 cm root of the parent tree (Diagram 89).

Mould foil around both trunks to 5 cm across. Bind with bonsai tape and texture.

Plant the tree by using one of the basic techniques, placing the trunk to one side of the container. I rather liked the look of a teak salad bowl for this bonsai.

Fill up any space in the bowl with plaster, paint it brown and sprinkle with a layer of cork granules.

Use a little brown texturing powder on the tree and stick pieces of brown reindeer moss around the roots and up the trunk.

The completed apricot should measure about 50 cm high from the table top.

WISTERIA (*FUJI*)
Literati style (*bunjingi*)

Materials

1.5 m Roman Bensilky No. 84
0.5 m Bensilky No. 38
1 m Bensilky Green No. 29
1 m Bensilky Green No. 5
Wires in gauges 18, 22, 30 and 26 lime green, 28 covered
Stem tape – nile and olive green
Bonsai tape – grey (2 rolls)
5 mm double-sided tape + glue or paste
Texturing materials

Flowers and Buds

Petals

Cut the roman silky into 3.6 cm squares and cut the lighter squares as pattern in Diagram 90.

Cut the darker squares as pattern in Diagram 91. Roll and cup the petals where marked on the diagram, or tool with a flower iron using the plain foot.

Cut some of the plain silky No. 38 into 8 pieces each 1.8 cm square, shape as Diagram 90 and put on one side for the buds. Cut the rest into 2.4 cm squares and shape as Diagram 90.

Assembling the large florettes (Diagram 92)

Take a 2.4 cm petal and fold in half within a 3.6 cm dark petal. Twist wire at the base, taking a small allowance, trim one wire off short and leave the other one about 8 cm long. Tape with a minimum of third-width nile tape.

Take a 3.6 cm light petal (curl outwards) and place behind the dark petal. Twist wire again, trim one wire short and tape in nile green.

Make 41 florettes.

Assembling the large bud florettes

Take a 2.4 cm petal and fold in half within a 3.6 cm dark petal as you did for the large

DIA. 90

DIA. 91

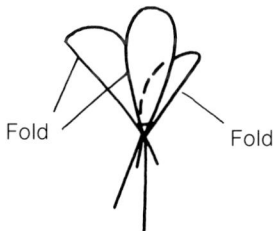

DIA. 92

DIA. 93

16 Wisteria (*height 50 cm*)

DIA. 94   DIA. 95

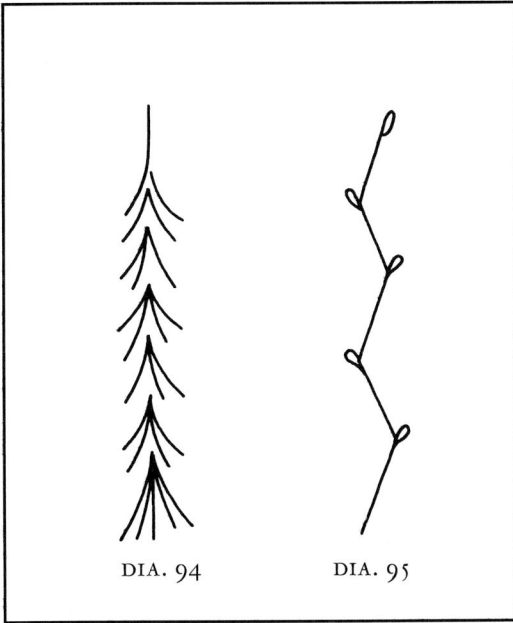

Work up the stem to the measurements given for each raceme, taping on 3 or 4 units at a time and varying the length of the stem so that the florettes overlap.

The open side of the florette should face outwards.

Large raceme –	5 small buds	
	3 medium buds	
	2 large florette buds	21 cm
	17 large florettes	
Medium raceme –	4 small buds	
	3 medium buds	
	2 large florette buds	18 cm
	13 large florettes	
Small raceme –	3 small buds	
	2 medium buds	
	2 large florette buds	16 cm
	11 large florettes	

florette. Twist wire at the base, leave a stem of about 8 cm and tape in third-width nile tape.

Tape on a calyx made from a 1.8 cm square of green silky No. 29 cut to shape as Diagram 93.

Make 6 large buds.

Assembling the medium florettes
Take a 1.8 cm petal and fold in half within a 2.4 cm petal.

Twist wire at the base, leave an 8 cm stem and tape in third-width nile tape. Tape on a calyx as in the large bud.

Make 8.

The smallest buds
These are made from scraps of ribbon rolled into a small cone. Twist wire, leaving an 8 cm stem, and add a small calyx made from tape.

Make 12.

Assembling the flower racemes (Diagram 94)
First tape a full-length piece of 22 wire with half-width nile tape, then tape the small buds onto the end, varying the length of the stems.

New growth shoots (Diagram 95)
Cut 26 gauge wire into 28 cm × 2 cm pieces, tape with third-width nile tape. Tape a half-piece of 22 wire and tape on the small wire buds at intervals on alternate sides.

Make 6 shoots.

Leaves
Leaves are made by cutting off a piece of ribbon the length of the leaf required, and creasing it into the appropriate widths. Stick a piece of narrow double-sided tape down the centre of each section, peel off the backing and place a quarter-piece of 26 lime green wire on the tape. Cut to shape as shown in Diagram 96.

Texture by the handkerchief method, and tape the stems in nile green.

Table of leaflet sizes:

Size 1
For 2 large leaves make
  6 leaflets 1.8 cm × 4.5 cm
  12 leaflets 2.4 cm × 5 cm

Size 2
For 4 medium leaves make
12 leaflets 1.2 cm × 3.5 cm
24 leaflets 1.8 cm × 4 cm

Size 3
For 6 small leaves make
18 leaflets 1.8 cm × 4 cm
24 leaflets 1.8 cm × 4.5 cm

Make up compound leaves sizes 1 and 2 on half-pieces of taped 22 wire, using 3 smaller leaflets with 6 larger ones.

The top leaflet has a 1.5 cm stem and subsequent leaflets have 0.5 cm stems. Space the pairs of leaflets about 2 cm apart (see Diagram 97).

Size 3 leaf uses 3 smaller leaflets with only 4 larger ones. After the last leaflet has been added, tape the stems in olive-green stem tape.

Branches

Using half-width olive-green stem tape make up the branches as in the diagram. Join in a whole piece of 18 wire at the first joint and thicken each section a little before the next addition.

Branch A – Diagram 98.
1 new shoot + 1 size 2 leaf + 1 size 3 leaf.

Thicken for 7 cm to 0.9 cm across. Finish the section with bonsai tape and mark.

Branch B – Diagram 99.
1 size 2 leaf + 1 new shoot + 1 small flower raceme; add 2 size 3 leaves + 1 new shoot at measurements shown. Thicken for 5 cm to 0.9 cm across, finish with bonsai tape and mark.

Branch C – Diagram 100.
1 size 2 leaf + 1 new shoot + 1 medium flower raceme. Change to bonsai tape and add 1 size 3 leaf + 1 size 1 leaf at measurements shown. Thicken for 4.5 cm to 1.3 cm across, finish in bonsai tape and mark.

Branch D – Diagram 101.
1 size 3 leaf + 1 new shoot; add 1 size 2 leaf + 1 size 1 leaf + 1 large flower raceme at measurements shown. Change to bonsai tape and add 1 size 3 leaf + 1 new shoot.

Thicken for 7.5 cm to 1.3 cm across, finish in bonsai tape and mark.

The branches may be textured with short lengths of bonsai tape before continuing. Form the tape into a slightly spiral effect, and sprinkle lightly with grey texturing powder while still wet.

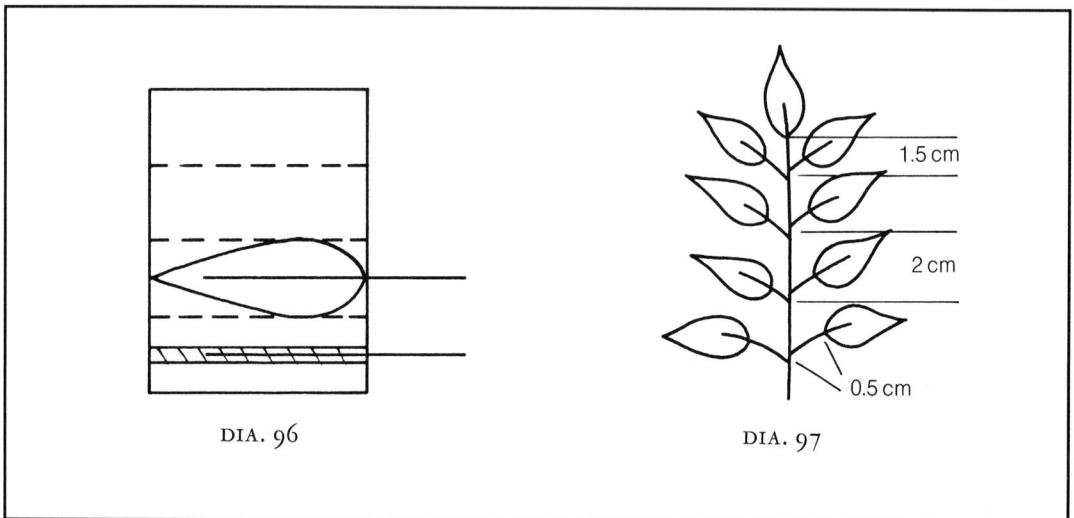

DIA. 96

DIA. 97

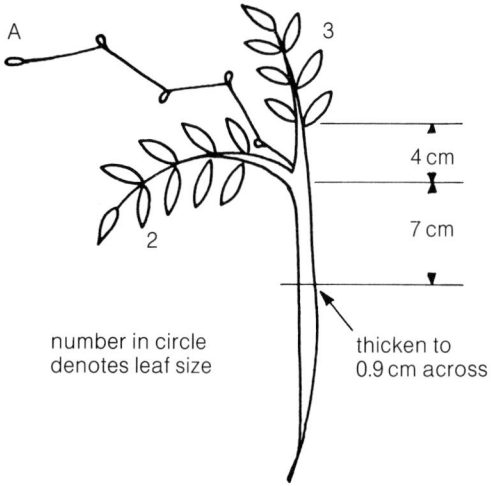

A

3

4 cm

7 cm

number in circle
denotes leaf size

2

thicken to
0.9 cm across

DIA. 98

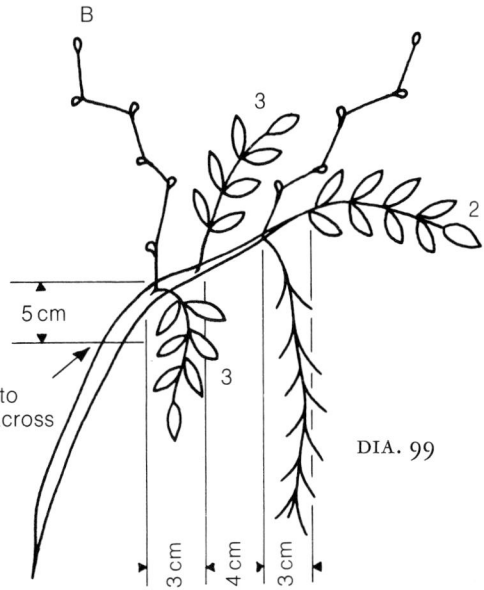

B

3

2

5 cm

thicken to
0.9 cm across

3

3 cm   4 cm   3 cm

DIA. 99

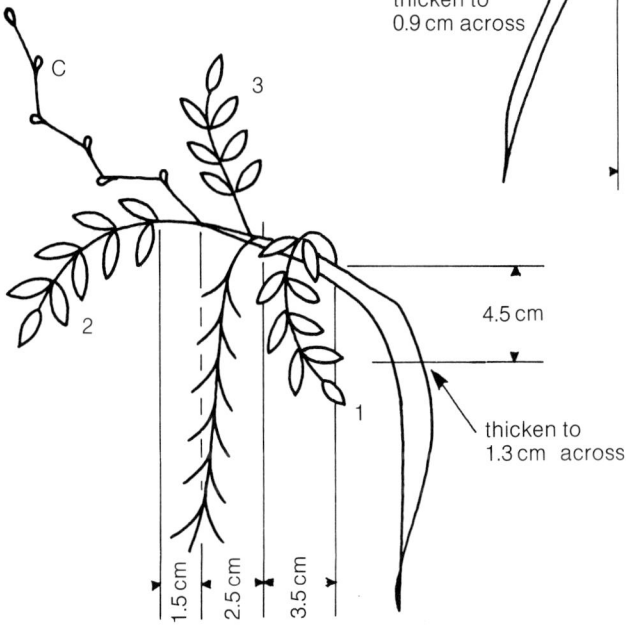

C

3

2

1

4.5 cm

thicken to
1.3 cm across

1.5 cm   2.5 cm   3.5 cm

DIA. 100

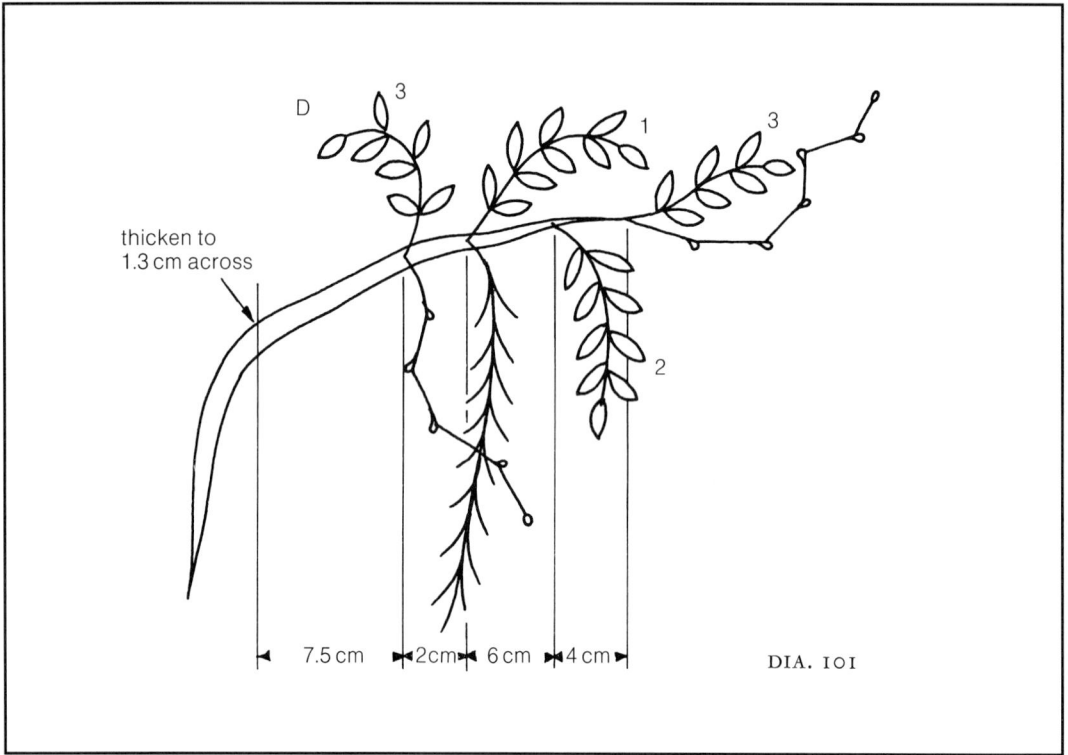

thicken to
1.3 cm across

D 3   1   3

2

◄ 7.5 cm ►◄2cm►◄ 6 cm ►◄4 cm►

DIA. 101

Roots and trunk (Diagram 102)
Using basic methods and following the measurements, make 2 divided roots and 2 single roots.

20 cm × 0.6 cm   Wire together 10 cm from
20 cm × 0.8 cm   the tips and tape with bonsai
                      tape for 3 cm

20 cm × 0.5 cm   Wire together 10 cm from
20 cm × 1 cm   the tips and tape with bonsai
                      tape for 2 cm.

1 root 20 cm × 1 cm
1 root 20 cm × 1.2 cm

Wire these 4 together so that the roots are 13 cm, 12 cm, 10 cm and 11 cm to the tips respectively.

Wire again 4 cm above the first wire, and then divide the trunk wires into 2 sections, one thicker than the other.

Tape each section firmly. Build up the thinner section with foil to 2.5 cm across at the base,

tapering off 18 cm above to 1 cm across, mark here and wrap the section with bonsai tape. Build up the thicker section with foil to 3 cm across at the base, tapering off 16 cm above to 2 cm across, mark here and wrap the section with bonsai tape.

Wire these 2 sections together on the marks, trim the excess wires to about 10 cm and tape firmly.

Bend and twist the trunk so that the thinner trunk on the left twists behind the thicker trunk and appears to join in on the right. Form a small elbow on the thinner trunk just below the joining point on the right side.

Now build up the base of the trunk in proportion to about 4 cm across. Take care with the shape, building up more on the left side to balance the slant of the trunk.

Assembling the tree (Diagram 102)
Wire together branches A and B, 7 cm below the last leaf on A, and 5 cm below the last leaf

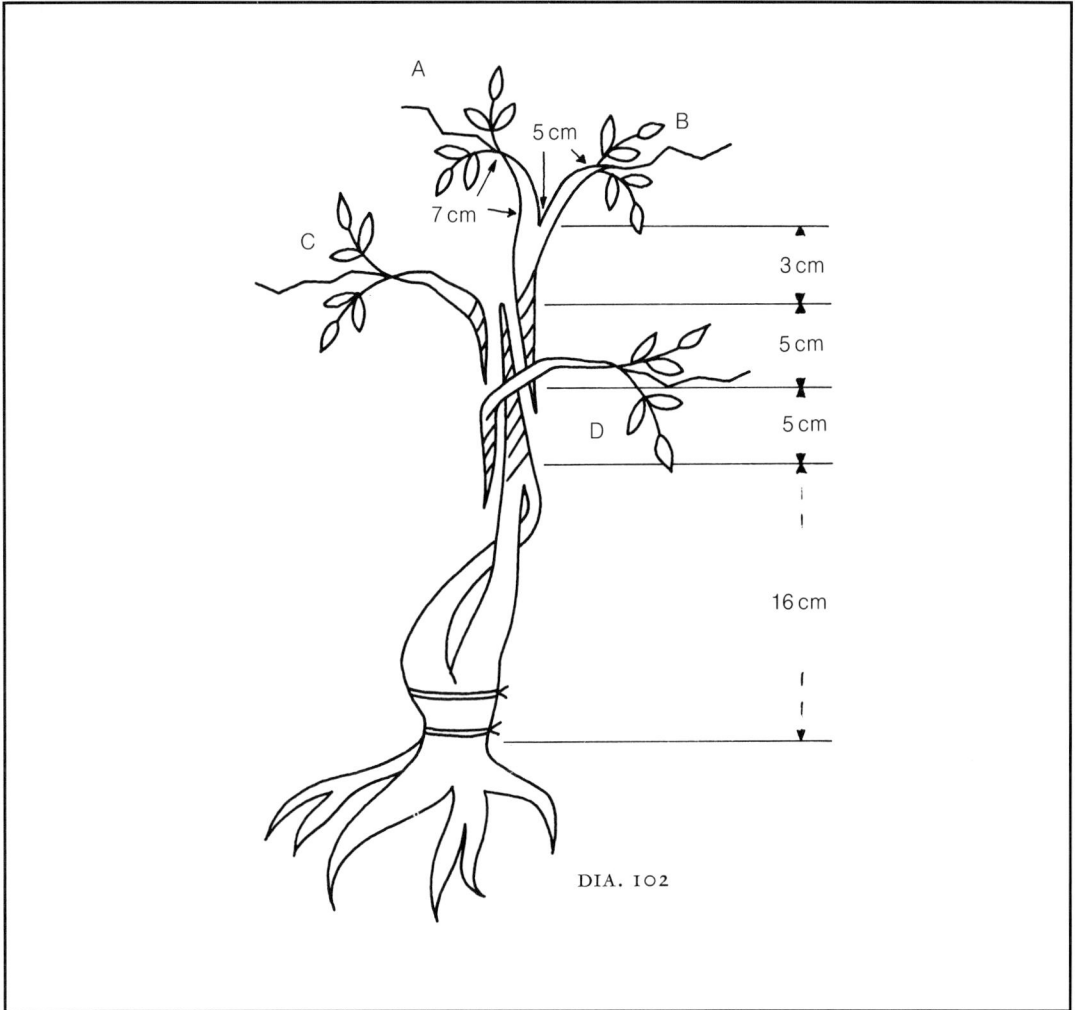

A

5 cm

7 cm →

B

C

3 cm

5 cm

D

5 cm

16 cm

DIA. 102

on B. Thicken for 3 cm to 1.5 cm across and finish in bonsai tape.

Join in branch C to the left and slightly forward.

Join all to the top of the trunk section, wire and tape firmly.

Thicken the trunk below the join for 5 cm to 2 cm across, finish in bonsai tape.

Join in branch D to the front and bend across to the right.

Thicken proportionately if necessary and texture the trunk, forming the bonsai tape into a spiral effect. Sprinkle while still wet with grey modelling powder.

Finishing touches
Plant the tree by one of the methods described before.

The bonsai dish I chose is an unusual octagonal shape in a dull green glaze.

Add some extra texture to the trunk with lichen powder and fill up the dish with moss. For a finishing touch, I added the delightful little toadstools I had found at a craft fair.

The wisteria will stand about 50 cm from the table top.

Useful information

Sources of supply
Hamilworth Floral Products Ltd
23 Lime Road,
Broadmeadow Estate
Dumbarton
Dunbartonshire
Scotland G82 2RP

Other stamens, berries and flock powder can
be obtained from
The Studio of Dorothea Richards
Merchants House
High Street
Bishops Waltham
Hampshire

Flock powder and texturing materials can
often be found in a model railway shop.

Reference books
Ribbon Flowermaking (from Hamilworth).
Horticultural books on bonsai are available at
  most libraries.

Courses in bonsai and silk flowermaking
Patricia Ratcliffe
Cedarvale School of Handmade Flowers
6 Peasholm Crescent
Scarborough
North Yorkshire YO12 7QX

Index

Page numbers in italic refer to illustrations.